DAILY SUMMER ACTIVITIES

BETWEEN GRADES 1 AND 2

Writing: Jo Ellen Moore
Content Editing: Marilyn Evans
Copy Editing: Cathy Harber
Art Direction: Cheryl Puckett
Cover Design: Liliana Potigian
Illustration: Jo Larsen
Design/Production: Cheryl Puckett
Michelle Tapola

EMC 1028

Evan-Moor®
EDUCATIONAL PUBLISHERS
Helping Children Learn since 1979

Visit
teaching-standards.com
to view a correlation
of this book.
This is a free service.

**Correlated to State and
Common Core State Standards**

**Congratulations on your purchase of some of the
finest teaching materials in the world.**

*No part of this book may be reproduced
in any form or stored in any retrieval system
without the written permission of publisher.*

For information about other Evan-Moor products, call 1-800-777-4362,
fax 1-800-777-4332, or visit our Web site, www.evan-moor.com.
Entire contents © 2005 EVAN-MOOR CORP.
18 Lower Ragsdale Drive, Monterey, CA 93940-5746. Printed in USA.

CPSIA: Hess Print Solutions, 3765 Sunnybrook Road, Brimfield, OH 44240 [03/2013]

Contents

Skills

Skills	Week									
	1	2	3	4	5	6	7	8	9	10
Reading Comprehension										
Following Directions	●	●	●	●						
Sequencing Events				●						
Who, What, Where, When?	●	●	●	●	●	●	●		●	●
Real/Make-Believe		●						●		
Inference		●				●		●		
Fluency	●	●		●	●	●		●	●	●
Grammar/Usage/Mechanics										
Phonics	●	●	●	●	●	●	●	●	●	●
Spelling	●	●	●	●	●	●	●	●	●	●
Alphabetical Order	●			●					●	●
Contractions		●								
Possessives										●
Plurals					●		●			
Parts of Speech		●		●						
Double Negatives					●					
Subject/Verb Agreement	●			●	●	●	●	●	●	●
Abbreviations									●	●
Capitalization	●	●	●	●	●	●	●	●	●	●
Punctuation	●	●	●	●	●	●	●	●	●	●
Vocabulary Development										
Rhyming Words	●					●		●		
Synonyms/Antonyms			●		●					
Homophones									●	
Comparatives/Superlatives		●								
Compound Words								●		
Writing										
Write a Sentence	●	●	●	●	●	●	●	●	●	●
Write a Paragraph									●	
Journal Writing	●	●	●	●	●	●	●	●	●	●

©2005 by Evan-Moor Corp. • Daily Summer Activities 1-2 • EMC 1028

Skills	Week 1	2	3	4	5	6	7	8	9	10
Handwriting										
Letters	●	●	●		●	●	●	●	●	●
Copy Text	●	●	●	●	●	●	●	●	●	●
Numbers				●						
Math										
Sequencing	●	●	●		●		●		●	
Number Words						●		●	●	
Word Problems	●	●	●	●	●	●	●	●	●	●
Tell Time					●					
Shapes	●		●	●			●	●	●	●
Money		●						●		●
Counting to 20/50/100	●	●			●	●				●
Place Value						●				●
Addition	●	●			●		●		●	
Column Addition/Subtraction		●	●	●		●		●	●	●
Subtraction	●	●	●		●	●		●	●	
Patterning	●		●	●		●				
Graphs and Grids		●	●	●						●
Ordinals								●		
Fractions		●					●			
Measurement					●	●		●		
Greater Than/Less Than/Equal to				●						
Geography										
Map Reading Skills					●	●		●	●	●
Directions	●			●						
Map Grids		●		●						
Compass Rose			●							
Globes							●			
Legends									●	

About This Book

What's in It

Ten Weekly Sections

Each section contains half-page and full-page activities that help children learn reading, writing, math, geography, spelling, grammar, and critical-thinking skills.

Each week, your child will work on the following:

Reading	▶ comprehension activities that include fiction and nonfiction topics
Spell It!	▶ an activity to practice the week's spelling words
Write It Right	▶ an editing activity to correct errors in spelling, grammar, and punctuation
Handwriting	▶ a writing activity to practice penmanship skills
Phonics and Language	▶ activities reviewing basic phonics and language rules, including vowels and consonants, parts of speech, and rhyming
Math Time	▶ activities that practice sequencing, computation, and word problems
In My Own Words	▶ creative-writing exercises
Finding My Way Around	▶ a map activity that tests beginner geography concepts
Problem Solving	▶ a critical-thinking activity
What Happened Today?	▶ a place to record a memorable moment from the week, and a reading log to record the number of minutes spent reading each day

©2005 by Evan-Moor Corp. • Daily Summer Activities 1-2 • EMC 1028

How to Use It

The short practice lessons in *Daily Summer Activities* prepare your child for the coming school year by making sure that he or she remembers all of the skills and concepts learned in first grade. After completing the activities in this book, your child will feel more confident as he or she begins the new school year. You can help your child by following the suggestions below.

Provide Time and Space

Make sure that your child has a quiet place for completing the activities. The practice session should be short and positive. Consider your child's personality and other activities as you decide how and where to schedule daily practice periods.

Encourage and Support

Your response is important to your child's feelings of success. Keep your remarks positive and recognize the effort your child has made. Correct mistakes together. Work toward independence, guiding practice when necessary.

Check in Each Week

Use the weekly record sheet to talk about the most memorable moments and learning experiences of the week and to discuss the books you are reading with your child.

Be a Model Reader

The most important thing you can do is to make sure your child sees you reading. Read books, magazines, and newspapers. Visit libraries and bookstores. Point out interesting signs, maps, and advertisements wherever you go. Even though your child is an independent reader, you can still share the reading experience by discussing what you read every day.

Go on Learning Excursions

Learning takes place everywhere and through many experiences. Build learning power over the summer by:

- visiting a zoo or a local children's museum.

- collecting art materials and working together to create a collage, mobile, or scrapbook.

- planning a calendar of summer events. Check off each event as you complete it.

- planting a garden. If you are short on space, plant in containers.

- visiting an older relative. Talk about his or her experiences when he or she was younger. Ask how things are different now.

- going grocery shopping together. Note foods or beverages that begin with a certain sound.

Spell It! This list contains all of the weekly spelling words practiced in the book.

A
all
and
ask

B
be
because
been
black
bone
box
bring
brown

C
came
clown
cute

D
doing

F
fast
find
for
funny

G
gave
going
green

H
happy
has
have
help
her
here
hill
home

J
jump

L
letter
like
little

M
make
making
messy
most
my

N
next
nine
no

P
puppy

R
ride
running

S
said
see
she
shop
silly
sing
sitting
sleep
small
smile
smiling
some
sunny

T
tell
the
time
to
two

U
use

W
want
was
we
went

Y
yellow

Z
zoo

Color a  for each page finished.

Parent's Initials

Monday

Tuesday

Wednesday

Thursday

Friday

_____

_____

_____

_____

_____

Spelling Words

her	nine
tell	we
for	green

What Happened Today? Write about one thing you did each day.

Monday _____

_____

Tuesday _____

_____

Wednesday _____

_____

Thursday _We went to the Weymouth_
club.

Friday _We will go to the Weymouth club_
dinner camp.

Keeping Track Color a book for every 10 minutes you read.

Monday	Tuesday	Wednesday	Thursday	Friday

My favorite book this week was

_____

I liked it because _____

_____

_____

©2005 by Evan-Moor Corp. • Daily Summer Activities 1-2 • EMC 1028

Bedtime

It's time to go to bed.
I put on my pajamas.
I brush my teeth.
I get my bunny.
I hop into bed.

Dad tucks me in.
He says,
"Good-night.
Sleep tight.
Don't let the bed bugs bite."

---

1. What did the child take to bed?

    bear   (bunny)   book

2. What did Dad do?

    read a story   tucked me in   kissed me

3. Circle what you do at bedtime.

    take a bath   (put on pajamas)
    wash my face   (read a book)
    (brush my teeth)   hide under the bed
    go outside to play   say a prayer

Write It Right

1. tony and maria are not home yet

Tony

2. she sung a funny song

She sang a funnysong.

3. did their team wore blue shirts

Did their team ware blue shirts

MATH TIME

Add and subtract.

2 + 1 = 3	5 - 5 = 0	2 - 1 = 1	2 - 0 = 2
0 + 2 = 2	2 + 3 = 5	1 + 3 = 4	1 + 1 = 2
4 - 3 = 1	4 + 1 = 5	4 - 2 = 2	5 - 4 = 1
2 + 2 = 4	3 - 2 = 1	5 - 3 = 2	5 - 2 = 3
5 - 1 = 4	5 + 0 = 5	3 + 2 = 5	3 + 1 = 4

©2005 by Evan-Moor Corp. • Daily Summer Activities 1–2 • EMC 1028

Spell It!

Write the spelling words in the boxes.

| her | nine | tell | we | for | green |

tell   her   we

nine   for   green

Write the missing spelling words in the sentences.

1. Jan took _____ her _____ little sister to the park.

2. I will be _____ nine _____ years old on Sunday.

3. Is your jacket _____ green _____ or yellow?

4. When can _____ we _____ go to the ball game?

Trace and write these lines and circles using your best handwriting.

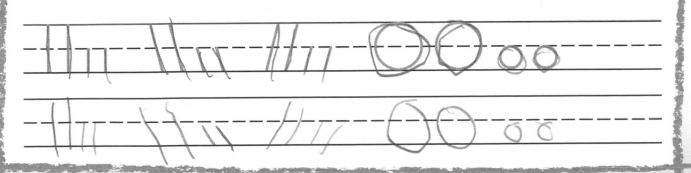

Tuesday

Week 1

13

©2005 by Evan-Moor Corp. • Daily Summer Activities 1-2 • EMC 1028

Letters–Sounds–Words–Letters

Write the missing consonant sound.

__b__ed   __d__uck   __H__at   __M__onkey

__C__oat   __W__agon   __P__urse   __Z__ebra

MATH⊙TIME

Write the numbers to 20.

1	2	3	4	5	6	7 8	9	10
11	12	13	14	15	16	17	18	19	20

Write the missing numbers.

__8__ 9 __10__   __16__ 11 __12__   __7__ 8 __9__

__3__ 4 __5__   __18__ 19 __20__   __14__ 15 __16__

__1__ 2 __3__   __15__ 16 __17__   __16__ 17 __18__

__6__ 7 __8__   __12__ 13 __14__   __11__ 12 __13__

(14)   Week 1   Tuesday

©2005 by Evan-Moor Corp. • Daily Summer Activities 1-2 • EMC 1028

How to Be Healthy

Do you want to grow big and strong?
Then you need to do these things:

★ Eat food that is good for you.

★ Wash your hands before you eat.

★ Wash your hands after you go to the bathroom.

★ Brush and floss your teeth after you eat.

★ Run and play every day.

★ Get rest and sleep.

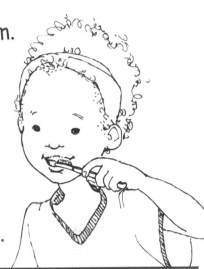

Do these things and you will stay healthy.

Make a line under the things in the list that you do.

Draw yourself:

| eating good food | running | washing your hands |

Match the pictures that rhyme.

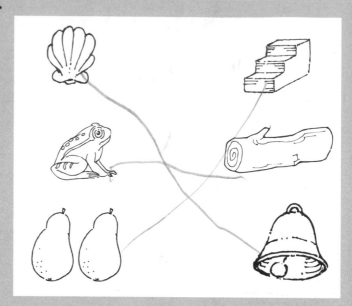

MATH⊙TIME

How many bugs?

1. I see 5 red bugs and 3 yellow bugs.
   How many bugs in all?

   _____8_____ bugs

2. I see 8 black bugs and 4 green bugs.
   How many more black bugs than green bugs?   _____4_____ bugs

3. I see 6 bugs. 4 more come.
   How many bugs in all?   6+4=

   _____10_____ bugs

4. I see 9 bugs. 3 bugs go away.
   How many bugs are left?

   _____6_____ bugs

©2005 by Evan-Moor Corp. • Daily Summer Activities 1-2 • EMC 1028

Finding My Way Around

1. Start at the ⭐ .
   Go left. What do you see?

2. Start at the ⭐ .
   Go down. What do you see?

3. Start at the ⭐ .
   Go right. What do you see?

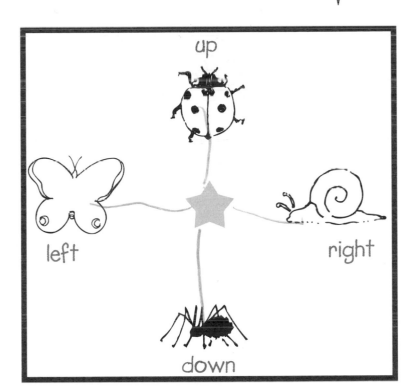

In My Own Words

Draw a snail in a garden.

Tell what the snail is doing.

He is sthnering to a flw.

©2005 by Evan-Moor Corp. • Daily Summer Activities 1-2 • EMC 1028

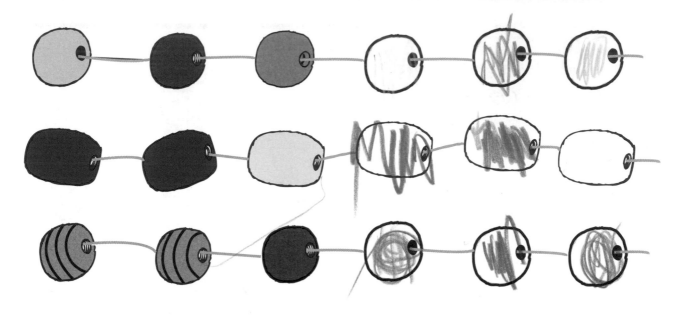

Letters – Sounds – Words – Letters

Fill in the letters of the alphabet that come before and after these letters.

a b c d e f g h i j k l m
n o p q r s t u v w x y z

b c d   W x y   f g h   g r s

l m h   e f g   c d e   i j k

x w y   p q r   q b s   d e f

©2005 by Evan-Moor Corp. • Daily Summer Activities 1-2 • EMC 1028

Read It!

Read these short vowel words to an adult.

fog	leg	yak	run	hid	zap
nut	rim	pen	rip	hat	cob
bud	tap	wig	not	fin	hot
nap	jug	lox	but	can	net
fat	job	pod	hem	lid	tub
yam	hen	bun	map	sip	tax
pot	men	fix	sun	box	cut

I can read all of these words. (yes) no

MATH TIME

Count the sides and corners.

___4___ sides
___4___ corners

___3___ sides
___3___ corners

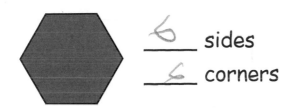

___6___ sides
___6___ corners

___4___ sides
___4___ corners

Name these shapes for an adult.

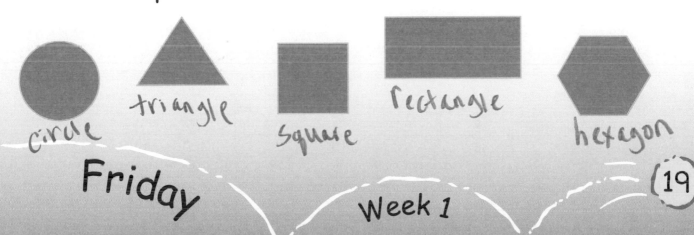

circle   triangle   square   rectangle   hexagon

Friday

Week 1

(19)

©2005 by Evan-Moor Corp. • Daily Summer Activities 1-2 • EMC 1028

My Robot

Connect my numbers from 1 to 20.

Color me.

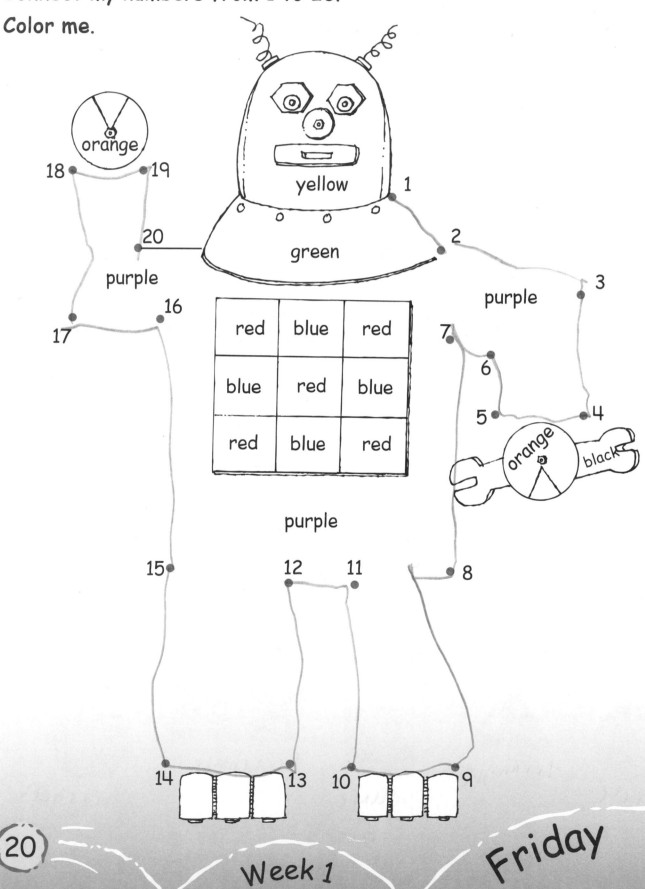

red	blue	red
blue	red	blue
red	blue	red

©2005 by Evan-Moor Corp. • Daily Summer Activities 1-2 • EMC 1028

Color a  for each page finished.

Parent's Initials

Monday	☆ ☆	_____
Tuesday	☆ ☆	_____
Wednesday	☆ ☆	_____
Thursday	☆ ☆	_____
Friday	☆ ☆	_____

Spelling Words

has	was
box	and
the	all

What Happened Today? Write about one thing you did each day.

Monday _____

_____

Tuesday _____

_____

Wednesday _____

_____

Thursday _____

_____

Friday *We went to the Weymouth club*

Keeping Track Color a book for every 10 minutes you read.

Monday	Tuesday	Wednesday	Thursday	Friday

My favorite book this week was

_____

I liked it because _____

_____

_____

©2005 by Evan-Moor Corp. • Daily Summer Activities 1–2 • EMC 1028

Mud Pies

Lei and Kim like to make mud pies. The girls put dirt in a dish. They put water in the dirt. They stir to make mud.

Next, the girls put the mud in a pie pan. They set the pan in the sun to dry.

"Do you want some mud pie?" the girls ask Kim's father.

1. How do the girls make mud?

   mix rocks and water

   mix twigs and water

   (mix dirt and water)

2. Why do they set the mud pie in the sun?

   to get hard

   ~~to cook~~

   to get big

3. What will Kim's father tell the girls?

   "Yes, I want mud pie."

   "No, I don't want mud pie."

Why will he say that?

It is grows.

©2005 by Evan-Moor Corp. • Daily Summer Activities 1-2 • EMC 1028

Write It Right

1. can us get a hot pizza

Can we get a hot pizza?

2. i can do it more better

I can do it much better!

3. she gots a letter from uncle carlos

She got a letter from uncle carlos

MATH TIME

Find the answers.

8 + 1 9	5 + 3 8	2 + 6 8	4 + 5 9	2 + 7 9	0 + 7 7	4 + 4 8
3 + 6 9	7 + 2 9	8 + 0 8	3 + 5 8	6 + 3 9	5 + 5 8	3 + 7 10
1 + 8 9	3 + 4 7	9 + 1 10	4 + 5 9	3 + 3 6	4 + 2 6	3 + 4 7

©2005 by Evan-Moor Corp. • Daily Summer Activities 1-2 • EMC 1028

Spell It!

Write the spelling words in the boxes.

has   was   box   and   the   all

Write the missing spelling words in the sentences.

1. What _____ in that big _____?

2. Jim _____ two cats _____ a big dog.

3. Do _____ of _____ children have pets?

Write these letters using your best handwriting.

A E F H I K L M N T

V W X Y Z i k l t x y z

Fill in the missing letter.

bo**x**

10

te**h**

lo**g**

gu**m**

bu**s**

we**b**

ne**h**

cu**p**

lea**f**

MATH○TIME

Write the numbers 21 to 50.

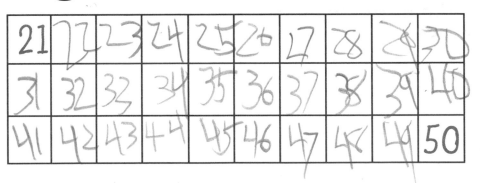

21	77	23	24	25	26	17	8	29	30
31	32	32	34	35	36	37	38	39	40
41	42	43	44	45	46	47	48	49	50

Unscramble these numbers.

35 37 34 38 36 33

33 34 35 36 37 38

©2005 by Evan-Moor Corp. • Daily Summer Activities 1-2 • EMC 1028

How to Make
MUD PIE

Here is how to make a mud pie you can eat. Make it with your mom or dad.

You need:

    1 gallon of soft chocolate ice cream

    2 cups of crushed Oreo® cookies

    $\frac{1}{4}$ cup of melted butter

Do this:

1. Mix the cookie crumbs and the butter.

2. Put the cookie crumb mix in a pan.
   Press it down to make a crust.

3. Put scoops of ice cream in the pan.
   Press the ice cream down with your hands.

4. Freeze the pie.

5. Cut a slice and eat it.

Why do you think it is called mud pie?

the chocolate looks like mud

How did you help make the pie?

all the steps.

Wednesday

A **noun** names a person, place, or thing.

Bob   park   shoe

Draw a circle around the nouns.

1. (Mom) put the (key) in the (car)

2. (Jose) got a blue (bike) and a red (helmet)

3. The (car) went down the (street)

4. (Anne) flew a (kite) at the (park)

5. That (dish) has ice cream in it.

Look around. Write the names of three things you see.

momey   _pilow_   _hisno wbox_

MATH◯TIME   Find the answers.

1. There are 5 white rabbits, 2 brown rabbits, and 3 black rabbits. How many rabbits are there in all?

_10_ rabbits

2. I see 4 rabbits. 5 more rabbits come. How many rabbits are there in all?

_9_ rabbits

3. 10 rabbits hop. 4 rabbits sit. How many more rabbits hop than sit?

10 — 4 =

_6_ rabbits

4. I had 8 rabbits. 2 rabbits ran away. How many rabbits do I have now?

_6_ rabbits

©2005 by Evan-Moor Corp. • Daily Summer Activities 1–2 • EMC 1028

Finding My Way Around

Start at the ⭐ each time.

1. over 3, up 2
   Draw a ♥.

2. over 6, up 4
   Draw a sun.

3. over 4, up 1
   Make an **X**.

4. over 2, up 6
   Draw an apple.

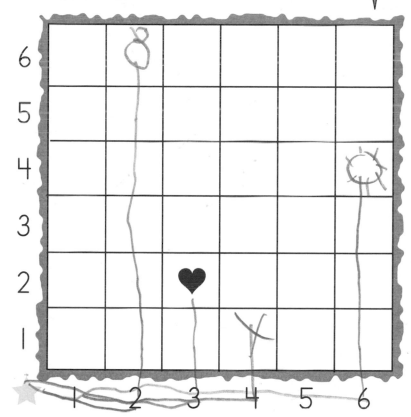

Draw a puppy with a bone.
Write a story about what
the puppy did with its bone.

the dog fohd q boneina hole.
the uk at e it k feel t happy

MATH●TIME

Count the money.

Match:

5¢   quarter

25¢   nickel

10¢   dime

1¢   penny

How much?

_45_ ¢   _30_ ¢   _13_ ¢

Letters – Sounds – Words – Letters – Sounds

©2005 by Evan-Moor Corp. • Daily Summer Activities 1-2 • EMC 1028

Match the words to the contractions.

cannot   isn't   I am   it's

is not   won't   he is   I'm

will not   can't   it is   he's

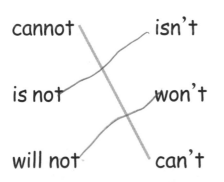
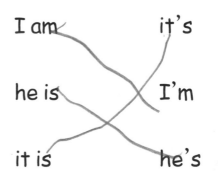

Read It!

Circle the color words.

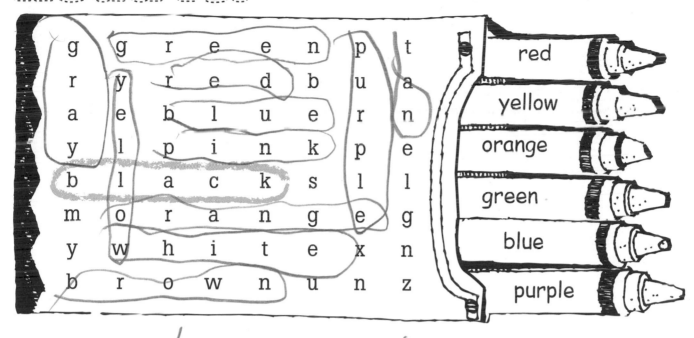

g	g	r	e	e	n	p	t
r	y	r	e	d	b	u	a
a	e	b	l	u	e	r	n
y	l	p	i	n	k	p	e
b	l	a	c	k	s	l	l
m	o	r	a	n	g	e	g
y	w	h	i	t	e	x	n
b	r	o	w	n	u	n	z

red
yellow
orange
green
blue
purple

black   brown   gray   pink   red   white
blue   green   orange   purple   tan   yellow

Read the color words to an adult.

MATH TIME

Circle the correct answers.

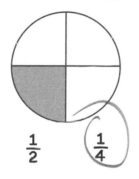 $\frac{1}{2}$ $\frac{1}{4}$

 $\frac{1}{2}$ $\frac{1}{4}$

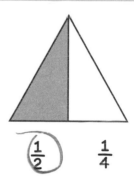 $\frac{1}{2}$ $\frac{1}{4}$

 $\frac{1}{2}$ $\frac{1}{4}$

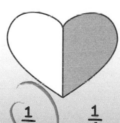 $\frac{1}{2}$ $\frac{1}{4}$

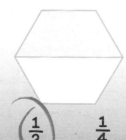 $\frac{1}{2}$ $\frac{1}{4}$

Friday

Week 2

(31)

Real or Make-Believe?

Color the things that are real.
Circle the things that are make-believe.

©2005 by Evan-Moor Corp. • Daily Summer Activities 1-2 • EMC 1028

Color a for each page finished.

Parent's Initials

Monday		_____
Tuesday		_____
Wednesday		_____
Thursday		_____
Friday		_____

Spelling Words

be	came
ask	ride
bone	cute

What Happened Today? Write about one thing you did each day.

Monday _____

_____

Tuesday _____

_____

Wednesday _____

_____

Thursday _____

_____

Friday _____

_____

Keeping Track Color a book for every 10 minutes you read.

Monday	Tuesday	Wednesday	Thursday	Friday

My favorite book this week was

_____

I liked it because _____

_____

_____

©2005 by Evan-Moor Corp. • Daily Summer Activities 1–2 • EMC 1028

Pet Day

It is show-and-tell day at school. The boys and girls can bring pets to class.

"This is my pet rat," said Carlos. "I give him seeds and fruit to eat. It is fun to have a white rat for a pet."

"This is my pet cat," said Lara. "She likes to sleep on my bed. It is fun to have a cat for a pet."

"This is my dog," said Tonya. "Sit, Gigi. Shake my hand. It is fun to have a dog for a pet."

"I don't have a pet yet," said Mike. "I can have a pet when we get a bigger house."

1. What can the boys and girls take to school?

    toys   treats   pets

2. Who has a pet white rat?

    Tonya   Carlos   Mike

3. What is Lara's pet?

    rat   dog   cat

4. When will Mike get a pet?

    when he is older   when he has a bigger house

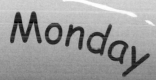
Monday   Week 3   35

©2005 by Evan-Moor Corp. • Daily Summer Activities 1-2 • EMC 1028

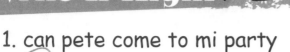
1. can pete come to mi party

   Canpete cometomyparty?

2. youll need boots and a hatt

   You'll need bootsandahat.

3. tell we all about you game

   Tell us about your game.

MATH⊙TIME

Find the answers.

7 - 2 *5*	8 - 4 *4*	9 - 7 *2*	7 - 3 *4*	8 - 8 *0*	10 - 6 *4*	9 - 4 *4*
6 - 2 *4*	8 - 7 *1*	7 - 7 *0*	10 - 5 *5*	8 - 2 *6*	9 - 6 *3*	9 - 2 *7*
10 - 4 *6*	9 - 3 *6*	7 - 5 *2*	10 - 1 *9*	7 - 4 *3*	6 - 3 *3*	8 - 5 *3*

Week 3

Monday

©2005 by Evan-Moor Corp. • Daily Summer Activities 1-2 • EMC 1028

Spell It! Write the spelling words in the boxes.

be   came   ask   ride   bone   cute

c a m e

c u t e

b e

a s k

r i d e

b o n e

Write the missing spelling words in the sentences.

1. Did Tomas _____ask_____ to _____ride_____ your bike?

2. I gave the _____cute_____ dog a big _____bone_____ to chew.

3. Maggie _____came_____ to my party.

4. Will you _____be_____ home if I come over?

Write these letters using your best handwriting.

C G J O Q S g j e

C G J O Q S g j e

C G J O Q S g j e

Write the missing short vowel sound.

a e i o u

w__e__b   s__i__x   s__u__n   c__a__t

p__i__g   b__o__x   c__u__p   r__a__t

MATH TIME

Write the missing numbers.

28	29	30
44	45	46
29	30	31

35	36	37
39	40	41
38	39	40

26	27	28
40	41	42
21	22	23

48	49	50
37	38	39
33	34	35

30	31	32
22	23	24
34	35	36

©2005 by Evan-Moor Corp. • Daily Summer Activities 1-2 • EMC 1028

Pet Care

You must take care of a pet. It needs food and water. It needs a place to sleep. It needs playtime, too.

You must be kind to your pet. Don't hurt it or scare it. Keep it safe.

If you go away, find someone to look after your pet.

1. What must you do to take care of your pet?

   It needs food water and a place to sleep.

2. What is the best kind of pet? Tell why you think it is best.

   A Dug is the best kihd of Pet it is the beth e case they like to Piay

Words that tell what you do are called **verbs**.

run   drive   work

Make a circle around the verbs.

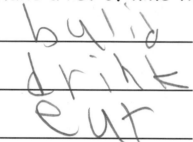 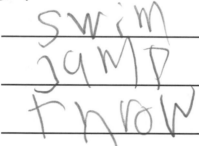

swim	green	sing	sleep
jump	chair	speak	coat
wink	play	catch	see
three	dive	paint	car

Make a list of nine things you can do.

bylid   swim   sleep

drink   jamp   cry

eat   throw   pee

 MATH TIME  **Find the answers.**

1. The clown had 9 balloons. He sold 5 balloons.
   How many did he have left?   4 balloons

2. There are 5 blue, 3 red, and 2 yellow
   balloons. How many are there in all?   10 balloons

3. I had 6 balloons. 3 balloons popped.
   How many do I have left?   3 balloons

4. I had 3 balloons. I got 6 more.
   How many do I have now?   9 balloons

Finding My Way Around ☀

A compass helps you find your way.
There are two kinds of compasses.

This is a compass you carry.
It always points north.

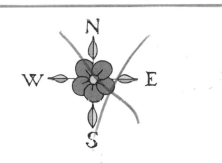

This is a compass on a map.
It points north, south,
east, and west.

1. Make a red X on the compass that is on a map.

2. Color the compass you carry green.

Number the pictures in order. Then tell about what happened.

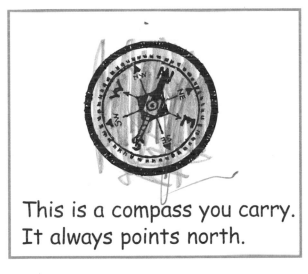

1 — Last the dog was clean

2 — Then the dog ggot a bath

3 — The dog got dirty first

MATH TIME — Larger and smaller.

Circle the larger number.

26   (34)

(95)   59

52   (73)

83   (86)

(48)   46

(11)   10

79   (97)

Make an X on the smaller number.

17   ✗15

✗50   70

31   ✗26

74   ✗47

✗89   98

23   ✗18

65   ✗39

Letters – Sounds – Words – Letters

Match the opposites.

happy   sad

tell — down
hard — ask
up — out
in — soft

come — cold
sad — small
hot — happy
big — go

©2005 by Evan-Moor Corp. • Daily Summer Activities 1-2 • EMC 1028

Read It!

Read these short vowel families to an adult.

an	met	it
can	bet	bit
fan	get	fit
man	let	hit
pan	met	lit
ran	net	pit
tan	pet	sit
van	set	flit
plan	jet	spit

I can read all of these words.   yes   no

MATH ● TIME

Color:

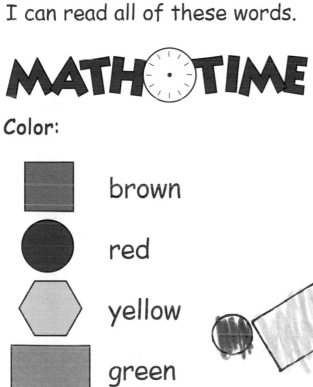

- brown
- red
- yellow
- green
- black

Look! Look!

Color the numbers hiding in this picture.

Week 3

Friday

Color a  for each page finished.

Parent's Initials

Monday   ☆ ☆   _____

Tuesday   ☆ ☆   _____

Wednesday   ☆ ☆   _____

Thursday   ☆ ☆   _____

Friday   ☆ ☆   _____

Spelling Words

see   she

shop   been

no   jump

What Happened Today? Write about one thing you did each day.

Monday _____

_____

Tuesday _____

_____

Wednesday _____

_____

Thursday _____

_____

Friday _____

_____

Keeping Track Color a book for every 10 minutes you read.

Monday	Tuesday	Wednesday	Thursday	Friday

My favorite book this week was

_____

I liked it because _____

_____

_____

©2005 by Evan-Moor Corp. • Daily Summer Activities 1-2 • EMC 1028

On Grandma's Farm

There is a nest on Grandma's farm.

There are some eggs
in the nest on Grandma's farm.

There is a hen sitting on the eggs
in the nest on Grandma's farm.

There are chicks that hatched from the eggs
in the nest on Grandma's farm.

Circle the answers.

1. Where did the hen lay her eggs?

    in a pen   in a barn   in a nest

2. What hatched out of the eggs?

    pups   chicks   bugs

3. The farm belongs to _____.

    Grandma   Grandpa   Father

Monday

©2005 by Evan-Moor Corp. • Daily Summer Activities 1-2 • EMC 1028

Write It Right

1. hes the biggest boy i ever seen

_____

2. max and me cant buy no popcorn

_____

3. we goes to the park every sunday

_____

MATH TIME   Find the answers.

$$
\begin{array}{c}
1 \\ 7 \\ +\,1 \\ \hline
\end{array}
\qquad
\begin{array}{c}
3 \\ 2 \\ +\,4 \\ \hline
\end{array}
\qquad
\begin{array}{c}
1 \\ 6 \\ +\,3 \\ \hline
\end{array}
\qquad
\begin{array}{c}
3 \\ 5 \\ +\,1 \\ \hline
\end{array}
\qquad
\begin{array}{c}
6 \\ 1 \\ +\,2 \\ \hline
\end{array}
\qquad
\begin{array}{c}
4 \\ 3 \\ +\,1 \\ \hline
\end{array}
\qquad
\begin{array}{c}
8 \\ 0 \\ +\,2 \\ \hline
\end{array}
$$

$$
\begin{array}{c}
2 \\ 5 \\ +\,2 \\ \hline
\end{array}
\qquad
\begin{array}{c}
3 \\ 4 \\ +\,3 \\ \hline
\end{array}
\qquad
\begin{array}{c}
5 \\ 2 \\ +\,3 \\ \hline
\end{array}
\qquad
\begin{array}{c}
6 \\ 1 \\ +\,2 \\ \hline
\end{array}
\qquad
\begin{array}{c}
5 \\ 2 \\ +\,1 \\ \hline
\end{array}
\qquad
\begin{array}{c}
7 \\ 0 \\ +\,2 \\ \hline
\end{array}
\qquad
\begin{array}{c}
2 \\ 6 \\ +\,1 \\ \hline
\end{array}
$$

©2005 by Evan-Moor Corp. • Daily Summer Activities 1-2 • EMC 1028

Spell It! Unscramble the spelling words.

see   she   shop   jump   no   been

1. ese ___see___

2. nebe _____

3. hes _____

4. hops _____

5. on _____

6. pujm _____

Fill in the missing spelling words in the sentences.

1. Did you _____ the horse _____ over the gate?

2. _____ put on green socks.

3. Have you _____ to the zoo?

Copy the numbers using your best handwriting.

1 2 3 4 5 _____

6 7 8 9 10 _____

one two three _____

Write the missing letters for the long vowel sounds.

a e i o u

f____ve   v____se   k____te   r____ke

b____ne   c____be   sn____ke   r____be

MATH TIME

10   20   ___   ___   ___

___   ___   ___   ___   ___

Count by 10s. Then connect the dots.

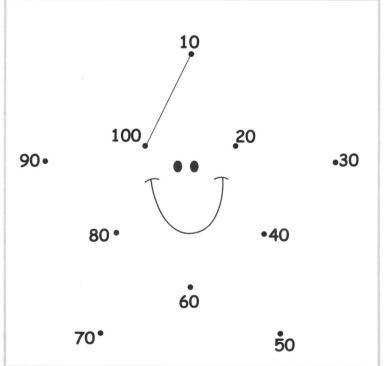

Week 4

Tuesday

©2005 by Evan-Moor Corp. • Daily Summer Activities 1-2 • EMC 1028

Bird Eggs

All kinds of birds lay eggs. Bird eggs may be small, or they may be big.

Bird eggs can be white or brown or blue. They can be round or oval.

But all bird eggs are the same in one way. Baby birds hatch from them.

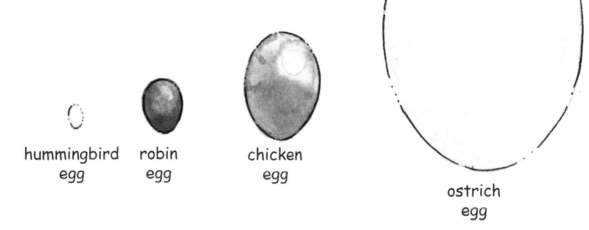

hummingbird
egg

robin
egg

chicken
egg

ostrich
egg

Number these pictures in order.

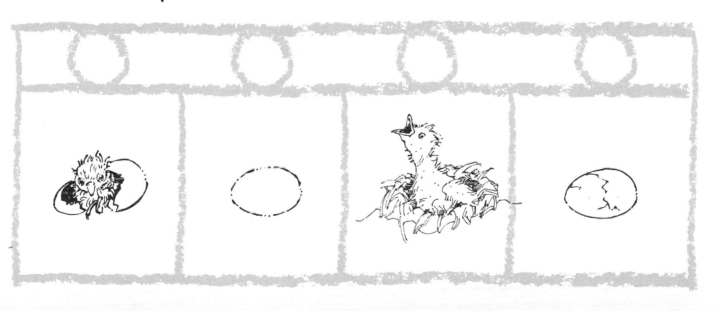

Write each set of words in alphabetical order.

a   b   c   d   e   f   g   h   i   j   k   l   m
n   o   p   q   r   s   t   u   v   w   x   y   z

box   apple _____

apple   _____

can   _____

elephant _____

duck   _____

fox   _____

mice   _____

chair   _____

zoo   _____

three   _____

six   _____

blue   _____

MATH TIME   Figure out how much fruit.

1. I saw 10 bananas in a bunch. 6 of the bananas
   were yellow. How many were still green?   _____ bananas

2. I have 5 oranges. I need 8 oranges.
   How many more do I need?   _____ oranges

3. I found 9 apples. 3 apples were red. 2 apples
   were green. How many apples were yellow?   _____ apples

4. I picked 6 pears yesterday. I picked 4 pears
   today. How many pears did I pick in all?   _____ pears

52

Week 4

Wednesday

©2005 by Evan-Moor Corp. • Daily Summer Activities 1-2 • EMC 1028

Finding My Way Around

Color the boxes to find your way through the maze.

1. go south 1
2. go east 2
3. go south 2
4. go west 2
5. go south 1
6. go east 3
7. go north 1
8. go east 2
9. go south 1

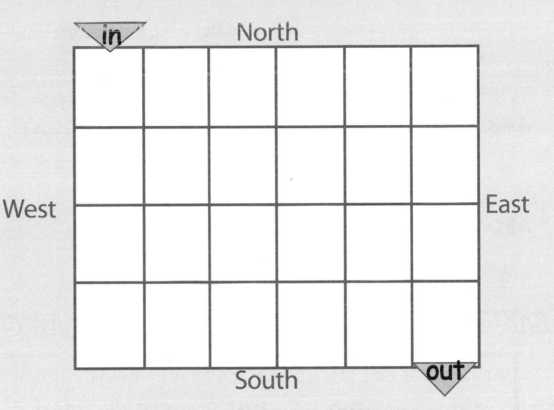

North

West

East

South

in

out

In My Own Words

Write a sentence that tells about this monkey.

_____

_____

Write a sentence that asks a question about this monkey.

_____

_____

Thursday

Week 4

53

MATH ⏰ TIME

Draw a pattern.

Example: ABAB _____ ⬜ ⚫ ⬜ ⚫ ⬜ ⚫

AABB _____ _____ _____ _____ _____ _____ _____ _____

ABCABC _____ _____ _____ _____ _____ _____ _____ _____

Letters – Sounds – Words – Letters – Sounds

Adjectives are words that describe things.

big   hot   six   red

Make a circle around the word that describes.
Then match the words and pictures.

ten dots
a (soft) cat

a fat frog
a tall hat

a wet mop
a red hen

©2005 by Evan-Moor Corp. • Daily Summer Activities 1-2 • EMC 1028

Read It!

An e at the end of a word can change a short vowel word to a long vowel word.

Add e to these words. Then read the words to an adult.

can can _e____   hop hop_____   Tim Tim_____

rip rip_____   cub cub_____   fin fin_____

bit bit_____   tap tap_____   rob rob_____

tub tub_____   kit kit_____   dim dim_____

MATH TIME

Greater than, less than, or equal?

6 (>) 3   4 (=) 4   2 (<) 5

5 ◯ 9   4 ◯ 3   16 ◯ 18

6 ◯ 2   7 ◯ 7   12 ◯ 11

15 ◯ 19   13 ◯ 12   19 ◯ 19

21 ◯ 12   24 ◯ 34   33 ◯ 22

30 ◯ 30   60 ◯ 90   100 ◯ 10

Friday   Week 4

 Crossword Puzzle

Across

1.

4.

5.

6.

8.

9.

Down

2.

3.

5.

7.

1 f	r	o	2 g

Word Box

| cow | goat | hen | pig | walrus |
| frog | goose | mice | sheep | whale |

©2005 by Evan-Moor Corp. • Daily Summer Activities 1-2 • EMC 1028

Color a  for each page finished.

Parent's Initials

Monday  _____

Tuesday  _____

Wednesday _____

Thursday  _____

Friday _____

Spelling Words

here	help
want	to
black	fast

What Happened Today? Write about one thing you did each day.

Monday _____
_____

Tuesday _____
_____

Wednesday _____
_____

Thursday _____
_____

Friday _____
_____

Keeping Track Color a book for every 10 minutes you read.

Monday	Tuesday	Wednesday	Thursday	Friday

My favorite book this week was

_____

I liked it because _____

_____

_____

©2005 by Evan-Moor Corp. • Daily Summer Activities 1-2 • EMC 1028

Lady AND Bubbles

Matt has two dogs. One is a big yellow dog. Her name is Lady. One dog is a frisky puppy. Her name is Bubbles.

Bubbles likes to play with Lady. Sometimes Lady gets tired of Bubbles. She growls and moves away. Bubbles will try to play with Lady again. Then Matt takes Bubbles to the front yard. At last Lady can get some rest.

1. Which dog is the biggest?

   Bubbles   Lady

2. What does Bubbles like to do?

   play with a ball   play with Lady   take a nap

3. How does Lady show she is tired of playing?

   growls   smiles   sleeps

4. Why does Matt put Bubbles in the front yard?

   to play with Bubbles   to let Lady rest

Monday

Write It Right

1. i runned faster than tanisha

_____

2. will you find the ball i losted

_____

3. my little brother cant never tie his shoes

_____

MATH⊙TIME

9 + 3 =	8 + 4 =	4 + 8 =
6 + 6 =	4 + 9 =	8 + 8 =
4 + 7 =	5 + 6 =	8 + 5 =
7 + 5 =	9 + 2 =	7 + 7 =
6 + 9 =	9 + 4 =	7 + 9 =
9 + 9 =	6 + 8 =	5 + 9 =

Week 5

Monday

©2005 by Evan-Moor Corp. • Daily Summer Activities 1-2 • EMC 102a

Spell It! Circle the correct spelling for each word.

here	help	want	to	black	fast

1. whant (want) wunt
2. balck blak black
3. hep help halp

4. to tew tou
5. heer here hree
6. fast fest fust

Fill in the missing spelling words in the sentences.

1. Can you come _____ and _____ me fix my bike?

2. I _____ a new _____ bike helmet.

3. I rode _____ the park as _____ as I could go.

Write your whole name using your best handwriting.

_____

- -

_____

Now write the first names of the people in your family.

_____

- -

_____

_____

- -

_____

©2C05 by Evan-Moor Corp. • Daily Summer Activities 1-2 • EMC 1028

Letters–Sounds–Words–Letters–Sounds

Write the beginning blend in these words.

| wh | sh | ch | th |

ch _____

_____ **30**

_____ _____ _____

_____ _____ _____

MATH TIME

Write the numbers from 51 through 100.

51	52								

Week 5

Tuesday

Dogs

There are many kinds of dogs. There are big dogs and small dogs. There are long dogs and short dogs.

Some dogs have ears that stand up. Some dogs have ears that hang down.

There are dogs with long tails, short tails, and no tails.

Dog hair can be long or short. There is even one dog with no hair! Dog hair can be one color. It can be more than one color.

Tell what each dog looks like.

Match words that mean about the same thing.

happy

glad

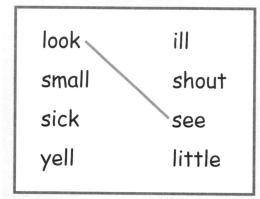

look	ill
small	shout
sick	see
yell	little

big	leap
jump	build
make	begin
start	large

MATH⊙TIME

How many pairs?

1. There are 2 mittens in a pair.
   How many mittens are in 2 pairs?

   _____ mittens

2. There are 2 socks in a pair. If I have
   10 socks, how many pairs do I have?

   _____ pairs

3. There are 2 shoes in a pair. Lee has
   3 pairs of shoes. How many shoes
   does he have?

   _____ shoes

4. I had 2 pairs of gloves. I lost 1 glove.
   How many gloves do I have left?

   _____ gloves

©2005 by Evan-Moor Corp. • Daily Summer Activities 1-2 • EMC 1028

Finding My Way Around

Draw a red line from the teacher's desk to the rug.

Draw a green line from the rug to the sink.

Draw a yellow line from the door to the window.

Draw an apple on the round table.

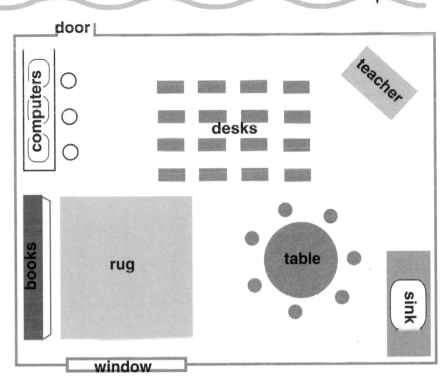

In My Own Words

I had a big surprise when I put my hand in my pocket. I found a
_____ in it!

It looked like this: _____

_____

It felt like this: _____

_____

I am going to _____

_____

Thursday

Week 5

©2005 by Evan-Moor Corp. • Daily Summer Activities 1-2 • EMC 1028

MATH TIME

4 : 00   ___ : ___   ___ : ___   ___ : ___

___ : ___   ___ : ___   ___ : ___   ___ : ___

Add **s** or **es** to the words to name more than one.

dog	watch
dog**s**	watch**es**

hat   _____   cake   _____

cow   _____   peach   _____

bench   _____   dish   _____

©2005 by Evan-Moor Corp. • Daily Summer Activities 1-2 • EMC 1028

Read It!

Read these words to an adult.

chill	where	she	think
chair	whale	shoe	thumb
chip	white	sheep	thorn
chicken	whip	shell	thread
cheese	what	ship	thin

I can read all of these words.   yes   no

 MATH TIME

Circle the tools used to measure things.

**Start at 51.
Connect the
dots to 100.**

59
61   60
62   58   100   99   98   97   96   95

57   94

63   93

56

64   51   55   92

52   90
54
53   91

71   73   89

65   72

70   74   88

66   68
67   80   81   82
69

75

79   83   87

76   77   78   84   85   86

This is an _____

It can _____

_____

©2005 by Evan-Moor Corp. • Daily Summer Activities 1-2 • EMC 1028

WEEK 6

Color a for each page finished.

Parent's Initials

Monday ☆ ☆ _____

Tuesday ☆ ☆ _____

Wednesday ☆ ☆ _____

Thursday ☆ ☆ _____

Friday ☆ ☆ _____

Spelling Words

small	yellow
letter	little
happy	silly
messy	hill

1. will you pushing she in the swing

   _____

2. he gots lots of candy

   _____

3. maurice taked his byke to school

   _____

MATH TIME

Use counters if you need help.

11 − 8	15 − 6	12 − 4	18 − 9	14 − 7	10 − 8
16 − 8	13 − 7	17 − 9	11 − 5	16 − 9	12 − 7
13 − 4	15 − 8	12 − 8	14 − 9	17 − 8	12 − 6

Week 6

Monday

©2005 by Evan-Moor Corp. • Daily Summer Activities 1-2 • EMC 1028

Spell It!
Circle the correct spelling for each word.

	small	yellow	letter	little
	happy	silly	messy	hill

1. smal   (small)   slam
2. happy   hapy   happe
3. leter   lettre   letter
4. messy   mesy   meesy

5. yelllow   yellow   yello
6. sille   sily   silly
7. hil   hill   hll
8. little   litlle   litul

Copy the names of the school days using your best handwriting.

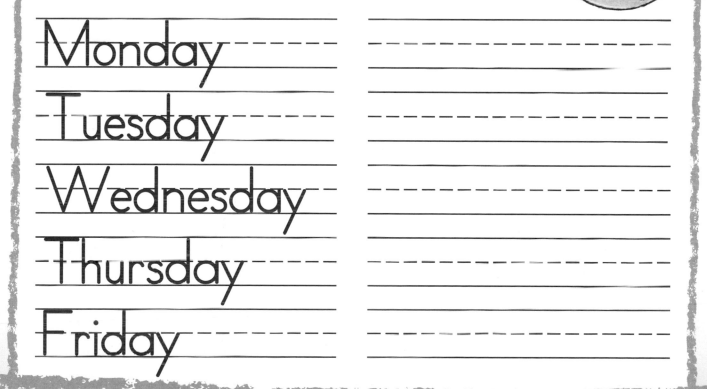

Monday _____

Tuesday _____

Wednesday _____

Thursday _____

Friday _____

Tuesday

Week 6

Letters – Sounds – Words – Letters

Fill in the missing letters.    **oa**   **ee**

b_____   g____t   j____p   t____d

f____t   s____p   c____t   tr_____

MATH TIME

Count by 5s to 100.

5	10	___	___	___
___	___	___	___	___
___	___	___	___	___
___	___	___	___	100

©2005 by Evan-Moor Corp. • Daily Summer Activities 1-2 • EMC 1028

Lizards

Lizards have scales on their skin. They have four legs. Their feet have long toes. Most lizards have long tails.

Lizards eat insects, spiders, and worms.

Lizards can run and climb.

Most lizards lay eggs. Mother lizards hide their eggs in sand or soft dirt. Lizard babies can run and find food as soon as they hatch.

Color the lizards.

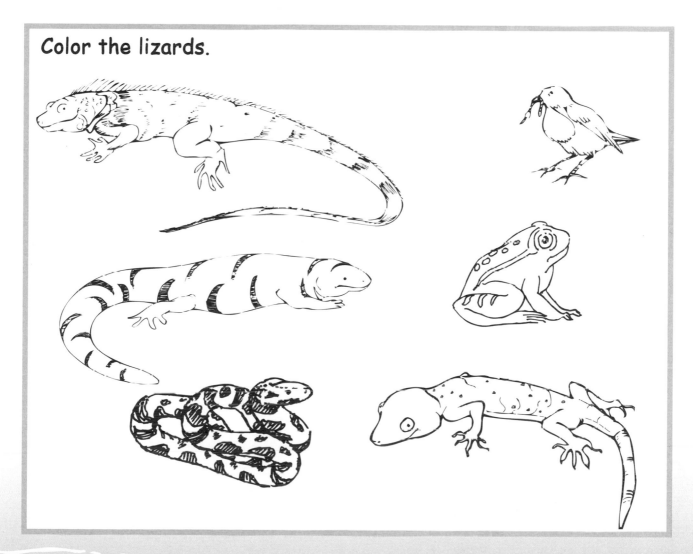

Write rhyming words in the sentences.

1. Jack and ___Jill___

   went up the ___hill___.

2. Little Bo _____

   has lost her _____.

3. Little Miss _____

   sat on a _____.

4. Hickory, dickory, _____

   the mouse ran up the _____ .

Word Box

Peep
hill
Muffet
sheep
clock
tuffet
Jill
dock

MATH TIME   Find the answers.

1. 10 kites went up in the air. 7 kites fell down.
   How many kites are still in the air?   _____ kites

2. 3 boys, 4 girls, and 1 teacher played a game.
   How many played the game?   _____ players

3. Will made 6 baskets and Mark made 4 baskets.
   How many baskets did they make in all?   _____ baskets

4. 9 children want to swing. There are 4 swings.
   How many children have to wait for a turn?   _____ children

Week 6

Wednesday

©2005 by Evan-Moor Corp. • Daily Summer Activities 1-2 • EMC 1028

Finding My Way Around ☀

This is Earth.
It is the planet we live on.

Color the land green.
Color the water blue.

In My Own Words

Write a letter to a friend. Tell your friend about something you did today.

Dear _____,

_____

_____

_____

Your friend,

_____

_____ inches

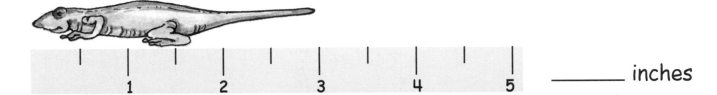

_____ inches

Letters – Sounds – Words – Letters

Pronouns are words that take the place of nouns.

He	**she**	**We**	**it**
They	**them**	**Her**	**us**

Write a pronoun on each line.

1. Dad has a box.   _He_ puts tools in _it_.

2. Mrs. Lee went to the store.   _____ son went to the store, too.

3. Stan and Will like to play ball.   _____ like to play ball.

4. Peter has a soccer ball.   _____ plays with _____.

5. Ann and I are going to school.   _____ are going to school.

Read It! Read these words to an adult.

the	a	A	for
they	from	of	to
you	with	I	this
that	was	are	have
by	all	how	said
were	as	your	or
The	want	draw	circle

I can read all of these words.   yes ☐   no ☐

MATH TIME   How many 10s and 1s?

29 = __2__ tens and __9__ ones

22 = _____ tens and _____ ones

37 = _____ tens and _____ ones

46 = _____ tens and _____ ones

A Number Word

Crossword Puzzle

Name the numbers.

Across	Down	Word Box	
1. 5	1. 4	eight	five
3. 2	2. 8	four	nine
5. 6	4. 9	one	seven
6. 3		six	ten
		two	three

©2005 by Evan-Moor Corp. • Daily Summer Activities 1-2 • EMC 1028

Color a  for each page finished.

Parent's Initials

Monday	☆ ☆	_____
Tuesday	☆ ☆	_____
Wednesday	☆ ☆	_____
Thursday	☆ ☆	_____
Friday	☆ ☆	_____

Spelling Words

going	doing
most	find
gave	next
have	went

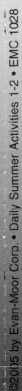

What Happened Today? Write about one thing you did each day.

Monday _____

_____

Tuesday _____

_____

Wednesday _____

_____

Thursday _____

_____

Friday _____

_____

Keeping Track Color a book for every 10 minutes you read.

Monday	Tuesday	Wednesday	Thursday	Friday

My favorite book this week was

_____

I liked it because _____

_____

_____

©2005 by Evan-Moor Corp. • Daily Summer Activities 1-2 • EMC 1028

A Lost Tooth

"Look! My tooth came out!" shouted Rosa. "I'm going to put it under my pillow. I hope the tooth fairy will come."

Rosa's teacher put the tooth in a small box. Rosa put the box in her pocket.

After school, Rosa ran to meet her sister. "My tooth fell out," she said. Rosa put a hand in her pocket to get the box. It was gone. She began to cry.

Just then, Jorge ran up. "You dropped this box," he said.

Rosa was so happy. She gave Jorge a big hug. "I will keep it in my hand," she said. "I don't want to drop it again."

1. What was Rosa going to do with her tooth?

_____

2. Why did the teacher put the tooth in a little box?

_____

3. Who found Rosa's tooth?

_____

4. How many teeth have you lost?

_____

Write It Right

1. dad and me goed fishing friday

_____

2. ellie hitted her head when she falled

_____

3. i found dads note in my lunch box

_____

MATH TIME

Find the answers.

62 + 36	71 + 18	82 + 15	93 + 3	25 + 24
45 + 52	61 + 37	17 + 82	97 + 2	48 + 51
23 + 12	45 + 34	32 + 56	81 + 17	22 + 33

©2005 by Evan-Moor Corp. • Daily Summer Activities 1-2 • EMC 1028

Spell It!

Unscramble the spelling words.

most	find	gave
next	have	went

1. dinf _____

2. xetn _____

3. toms _____

4. twen _____

5. vage _____

6. heav _____

Write a sentence using each of these spelling words.   **going   doing**

1. _____

2. _____

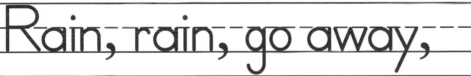

Copy this poem using your best handwriting.

Rain, rain, go away,
Come again another day.

_____

_____

_____

Tuesday

Week 7

85

Letters-Sounds-Words-Letters

Fill in the missing letters.　　　ai　　　ay

p_ai_nt　　　tr____n　　　h_____　　　j_____

r____n　　　cl_____　　　ch_____n　　　tr_____

Circle the words with the sound of a in say.

1. The hay is in the box.

2. The man spilled his paint.

3. It has started to rain.

4. Mother has a gray coat.

MATH TIME

Fill in the missing numbers.

51	52	53	___	64	___	___	90	___
___	68	___	___	87	___	___	62	___
___	80	___	___	77	___	___	81	___
___	99	___	___	69	___	___	56	___

©2005 by Evan-Moor Corp. • Daily Summer Activities 1-2 • EMC 1028

Teeth

When you are grown, you will have 28 to 32 teeth in all.

You need your teeth when you eat. Teeth tear and grind your food into small bits. Then you can swallow the food.

You must take care of your teeth. Brush and floss your teeth every day. Go to the dentist, too. Then you will have strong teeth.

1. How do teeth help you eat?

_____

_____

_____

2. What can you do to make your teeth strong?

_____

_____

_____

_____

_____

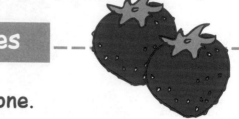

berry	berries

Drop the y and add ies to name more than one.

1. city _____   4. fairy _____

2. pony _____   5. cherry _____

3. baby _____   6. fly _____

Some words change to show more than one.

1. man _____*men*_____   3. tooth _____

2. mouse _____   4. foot _____

MATH TIME   Find the answers.

1. Ali took 10 cookies from the bag. He gave
   2 cookies to Marta. He ate 3 cookies.
   How many cookies are left?   _____ cookies

2. A frog ate 12 bugs. A toad ate 15 bugs.
   How many bugs did they eat in all?   _____ bugs

3. I gave my puppy six bones. He ate
   three bones. How many bones are left?   _____ bones

4. It is 5 o'clock. We are going to eat
   supper in 1 hour. At what time will
   we eat?   _____ o'clock

©2005 by Evan-Moor Corp. • Daily Summer Activities 1-2 • EMC 1028

Geography

This is a globe.

It is round like Earth.

We use a globe to find places.

Color the land green.

Color the water blue.

In My Own Words

Write a sentence that tells about this clown.

_____

_____

_____

Write a sentence that asks a question about this clown.

_____

_____

_____

Thursday

Week 7

MATH ⏱ TIME

Color $\frac{1}{2}$.

Color $\frac{1}{4}$.

Color $\frac{1}{4}$.

Color $\frac{1}{2}$.

Letters – Sounds – Words – Letters

Circle who is talking.
Underline what is being said.

(Lee) said, "I'll get us something to drink."

1. "Do you have a pet dog?" asked Mark.

2. Sumi shouted, "Keep away from that fire!"

3. "Why do I have to go to bed now?" asked Raul.

4. Will said, "I like to play ball with my friends."

5. Mike asked, "How soon will it be dinnertime?"

©2005 by Evan-Moor Corp. • Daily Summer Activities 1-2 • EMC 1028

Read It!

ee	oa	ai	ay
b __ee__	c____t	r____n	s_____
tr_____	g____t	g____n	w_____
s____n	cr____k	p____n	pl_____
thr_____	fl____t	w____t	cl_____
str_____t	c____ch	p____nt	st_____

MATH TIME

Find and mark the shapes.

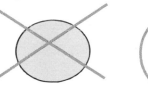

sphere   cone   cube

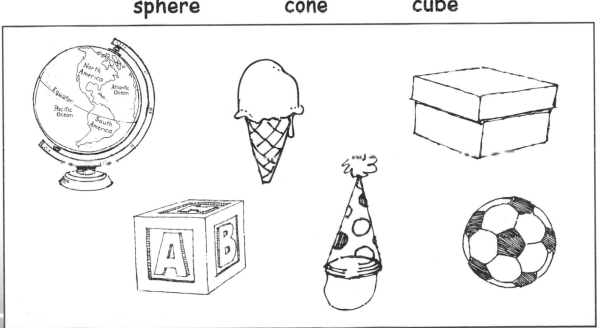

Friday

Week 7

91

Good to Eat

I'm hard as a rock when I go into the pot.
I'm fluffy and white when I get very hot.

What am I? _____

Draw and color the other side of the picture.

©2005 by Evan-Moor Corp. • Daily Summer Activities 1-2 • EMC 1028

Color a for each page finished.

Parent's Initials

Monday		_____
Tuesday		_____
Wednesday		_____
Thursday		_____
Friday		_____

Spelling Words

zoo	some
brown	home
funny	running
clown	sitting

1. her have red and blue ribbons

_____

2. when is you going two garys house

_____

3. abdul dont find nothing under his bed

_____

MATH TIME  Find the answers.

98 - 23	99 - 78	57 - 25	76 - 45	88 - 67
35 - 12	54 - 31	77 - 56	24 - 13	32 - 20
66 - 51	55 - 34	91 - 60	67 - 45	

Week 8

Monday

Spell It!

Find these spelling words in the word search.

zoo	some	sitting	home
funny	running	clown	brown

b c l o w n q s
r u n n i n g o
o z f u n n y m
w o x h o m e e
n o o m e z s i
s i t t i n g n

Write the two spelling words that rhyme.

_____   _____

Write your address using your best handwriting.

_____

- -

_____
house number and street name

_____

- -

city   state   zip

©2005 by Evan-Moor Corp. • Daily Summer Activities 1-2 • EMC 1028

A **compound word** is two small words put together to make a new word.

1. basket + ball ___basketball___

2. rain + bow _____

3. skate + board _____

4. pop + corn _____

Draw one new compound word.

MATH ⊙ TIME

Find the answers.

1. Mel asked seven friends to his party. Two didn't come. How many did come?

   _____ friends

2. Annie made five paper flowers. She made two of them red. She made the rest yellow. How many are yellow?

   _____ yellow flowers

3. Four bees flew to two flowers. How many more bees are there than flowers?

   _____ more bees

4. Tammy needed six cups. She got two from Sam and two from Penny. How many more cups does she need?

   _____ cups

©2005 by Evan-Moor Corp. • Daily Summer Activities 1-2 • EMC 1028

Ge✲graphy

This is a map.
A map is flat.
It shows places on Earth.

Color the land green.
Color the water blue.

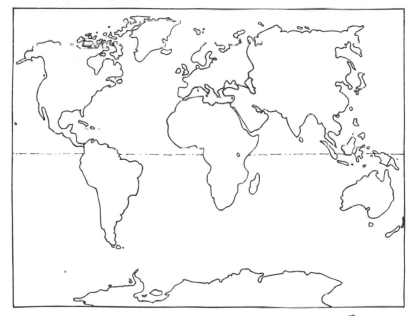

Write a List

Pretend you are going on a trip.
List what you would pack in your bag.

_____

_____

_____

_____

_____

_____

MATH TIME

_____ centimeters

| 1 | 2 | 3 | 4 | 5 | 6 | 7 | 8 | 9 | 10 | 11 |

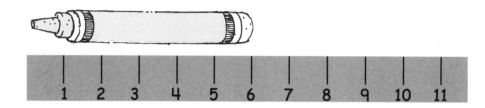

_____ centimeters

| 1 | 2 | 3 | 4 | 5 | 6 | 7 | 8 | 9 | 10 | 11 |

Letters - Sounds - Words - Letters

Circle the answers.

1. I get a can and take off
   the lid. I put food in a dish.
   I am feeding the...

   cat   fish

2. I made a mess.
   It is hard to clean up.
   I spilled...

   popcorn   honey

3. It is cold and wet.
   Rain comes down.
   I put on a...

   sun hat   raincoat

4. I get a rag and soap.
   I fill a tub of water.
   I am washing the...

   dog   house

(102)

Week 8

Thursday

©2005 by Evan-Moor Corp. • Daily Summer Activities 1-2 • EMC 1028

Read It!

book	cool	
look	tool	
hook	pool	
took	school	
crook	spool	
shook	stool	

Now can you read these?

wood	too
food	moon
soon	hood
stood	boot
zoo	good

I can read these words.

yes   no

I can read these words.

yes   no

MATH TIME

What does it cost?

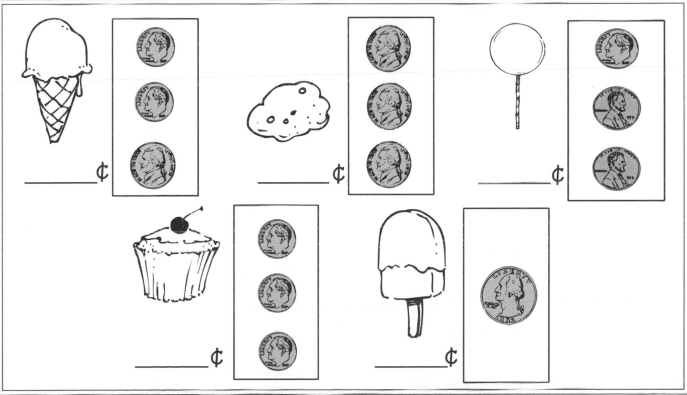

_____ ¢

_____ ¢

_____ ¢

_____ ¢

_____ ¢

The Cowboy

Draw and color the other side.

©2005 by Evan-Moor Corp. • Daily Summer Activities 1-2 • EMC 1028

Color a  for each page finished.

Parent's Initials

Monday	☆	☆	_____
Tuesday	☆	☆	_____
Wednesday	☆	☆	_____
Thursday	☆	☆	_____
Friday	☆	☆	_____

Spelling Words

make	two
making	use
smile	like
smiling	sleep

What Happened Today? Write about one thing you did each day.

Monday _____

_____

Tuesday _____

_____

Wednesday _____

_____

Thursday _____

_____

Friday _____

_____

Keeping Track Color a book for every 10 minutes you read.

Monday	Tuesday	Wednesday	Thursday	Friday

My favorite book this week was

_____

I liked it because _____

_____

_____

©2005 by Evan-Moor Corp. • Daily Summer Activities 1-2 • EMC 1028

Hay Ride

pickup truck

hay

wagon

Jim and Cody like to go to Uncle Elmo's farm. There are lots of fun things to do. The most fun thing is going on a hayride.

Uncle Elmo fills a big wagon with hay. He hooks the wagon to his pickup truck. All the kids get into the wagon. Off they go!

Uncle Elmo pulls the wagon to the river. The kids wade in the water. Then they eat a picnic lunch.

On the way back to the farm, they sing and tell jokes.

1. Why do Jim and Cody like going to Uncle Elmo's farm?

_____

2. What do the kids do at the river?

_____

3. What do the kids do on the way back to the farm?

_____

4. Why does Uncle Elmo put hay in the wagon?

_____

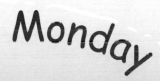

Monday

Week 9

Write It Right

1. sally hided the box inn the closet

_____

2. hes the most tall boy in our class

_____

3. torys more faster than we is

_____

MATH TIME

Find the answers.

23 + 34	22 + 46	68 - 42	27 + 72	91 - 71
55 - 34	54 + 25	73 + 16	99 - 83	28 + 71
39 - 3	59 - 36	52 + 42	42 + 32	98 - 26

Spell It!

Unscramble the spelling words.

make	two	smile	like
making	use	smiling	sleep

1. wot _____

2. sue _____

3. kame _____

4. miles _____

5. peels _____

6. keil _____

Write sentences using making and smiling.

1. _____

2. _____

Copy these words using your best handwriting.

Queen's quilt
_____

Frog's fat flies
_____

Zeke's zipper
_____

Letters–Sounds–Words–Letters

Fill in the missing letters.　　　　now　　　　mouth

cr_____n

c_____

sh_____t

h_____se

cl_____n

m_____se

MATH TIME

Count by 2s to 20.

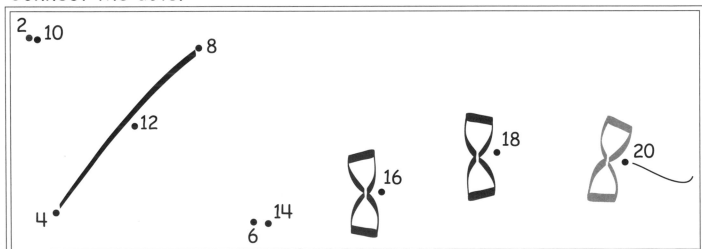

Connect the dots.

110　　　　Week 9　　　　Tuesday

©2005 by Evan-Moor Corp. • Daily Summer Activities 1-2 • EMC 1028

A Pickup Truck

People use pickup trucks when they work. A farmer hauls hay, feed, and animals. A carpenter hauls tools and lumber. A gardener hauls large and small plants.

A family may use a pickup truck when they move. The pickup can haul furniture and boxes to their new home.

People use a pickup truck for fun, too. They may use a pickup when they go camping. Horse owners may use a pickup truck to pull their horse trailers.

For work or for play, a pickup can be useful.

Circle the correct words.

Who is using the pickup truck?

1. The pickup is loaded with tents and sleeping bags.

   carpenter

   farmer

   camper

2. The pickup is loaded with plants, rakes, and shovels.

   gardener

   horse owner

   carpenter

3. The pickup is loaded with lumber, ladders, and hammers.

   farmer

   carpenter

   gardener

 How many ears do
6 otters have?

_____ ears

 How many arms do
4 sea stars have?

_____ arms

 How many tails do
3 seahorses have?

_____ tails

 How many arms do
2 octopuses have?

_____ arms

Letters–Sounds–Words–Letters

Write the correct word on each line.

ant
aunt

1. My _____ likes to bake cakes.

2. An _____ was in the cookie jar.

beat
beet

3. I _____ my sister in the bike race.

4. Dad planted _____ seeds in the garden.

break
brake

5. Mom stepped on the _____ to stop the car.

6. How did you _____ my toy?

Read It! Read these word families to an adult.

down	found	
gown	round	
town	pound	
brown	sound	I can read all of these words.
clown	hound	
frown	ground	yes no

MATH TIME

Write each number as a word.

1-one	2-two	3-three	4-four	5-five
6-six	7-seven	8-eight	9-nine	10-ten

six + one = __seven__   one + one = _____

ten - six = _____   two + three = _____

seven + two = _____   five - two = _____

six - five = _____   nine - three = _____

Friday

Week 9

115

Connect the dots from A to Z.
Now connect the dots from a to z.
Color the picture.

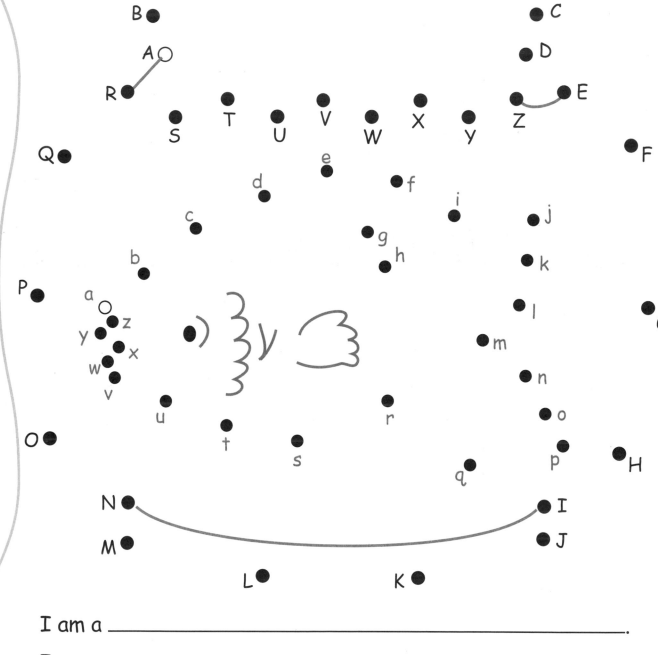

I am a _____.

I can _____.

Week 9

Friday

©2005 by Evan-Moor Corp. • Daily Summer Activities 1-2 • EMC 1028

Color a  for each page finished.

Parent's Initials

Monday ☆ ☆ _____

Tuesday ☆ ☆ _____

Wednesday ☆ ☆ _____

Thursday ☆ ☆ _____

Friday ☆ ☆ _____

Spelling Words

time	sing
my	bring
said	puppy
sunny	because

What Happened Today? Write about one thing you did each day.

Monday _____

_____

Tuesday _____

_____

Wednesday _____

_____

Thursday _____

_____

Friday _____

_____

Keeping Track Color a book for every 10 minutes you read.

Monday	Tuesday	Wednesday	Thursday	Friday

My favorite book this week was

_____

I liked it because _____

_____

_____

©2005 by Evan-Moor Corp. • Daily Summer Activities 1-2 • EMC 1028

Monkeys

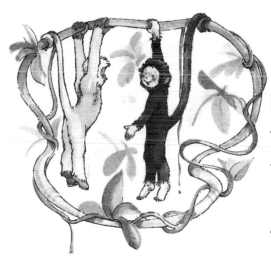

Jamal and his dad went to the zoo. They liked the monkeys best. It was fun to see them swing in the trees. They made funny faces at Jamal and his dad.

"I want a pet monkey," Jamal told his dad. "It can stay in my room."

"Wild animals are not good pets," said Dad. "Monkeys would make a mess in the house. And they need to be with other monkeys."

That night Jamal had a funny dream. He was a monkey! It was fun to swing in the trees. It was fun to make funny faces.

Circle the answers.

1. Where did Jamal go with his dad?

    the park   the farm   the zoo

2. What did the monkeys do at the zoo?

    swung in the trees   ate bananas   chased birds

3. Why did Dad tell Jamal he could not have a pet monkey?

    Monkeys could hurt him.

    Monkeys would make a mess in the house.

    Monkeys are good pets.

4. What did Jamal dream?

    He trained monkeys.   He could fly.   He was a monkey.

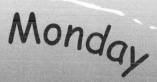

1. where does you live

_____

2. will you call mr martin for me

_____

3. i licked that book about them cowboys

_____

MATH TIME   Find the answers.

```
  41        21        61        12        34
  35        13         7        55        33
+ 23      + 64      + 21      + 11      + 22
```

```
  56        34        63        12        34
  11        51        15        23        42
+ 32      + 14      + 21      + 24      + 31
```

©2005 by Evan-Moor Corp. • Daily Summer Activities 1-2 • EMC 1028

Spell It! Circle the correct spelling for each word.

time	sing	my	bring
said	sunny	puppy	because

1. time   tim   teme

2. mu   mi   my

3. sed   said   siad

4. sunny   suny   sunney

5. seng   sing   signe

6. bring   breng   brige

7. puggy   puppe   puppy

8. becuz   because   decuase

Copy this sentence using your best handwriting.

Five jolly circus monkeys
zipped quickly around
that big wooden box.

Write the beginning sounds.

gl bl	sl gl	gl bl
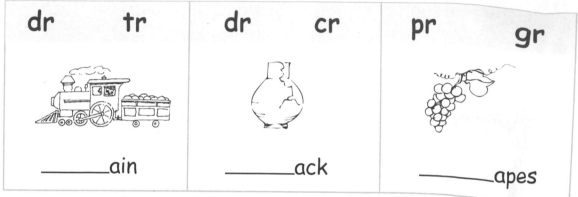		
_____ad	_____ip	_____ack

dr tr	dr cr	pr gr
_____ain	_____ack	_____apes

MATH⊙TIME

Find the answers.

10   1   10 + 1 = 11

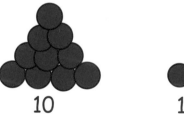 + 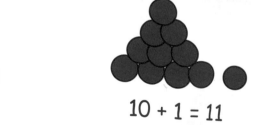 = ☐

 + 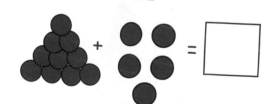 = ☐

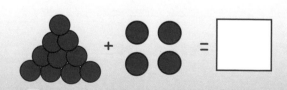 + ●●●● = ☐

 = ☐

Week 10

Tuesday

©2005 by Evan-Moor Corp. • Daily Summer Activities 1-2 • EMC 1028

Monkeys

Monkeys live in jungles. Jungles are very warm and damp. Many plants grow there. Monkeys live in the trees. They eat fruit and seeds from the plants.

Monkeys use their feet and hands to hold onto the branches. Some kinds of monkeys can hold on with their tails, too.

A baby monkey stays with its mother for many months. The mother feeds her baby. She keeps her baby safe from harm, too.

1. Where do monkeys live?

_____

2. What do monkeys eat?

_____

3. How do monkeys move in the trees?

_____

4. What does a mother monkey do for her baby?

_____

Use ' to show who owns something.

1. The ball belongs to Ted.

   ___Ted's___ ball

2. That truck belongs to the farmer.

   the _____ truck

3. The red coat belongs to Mary.

   _____ red coat

4. The tools belong to my father.

   my _____ tools

MATH⏰TIME

Find the answers.

1. Three cows are in the field. How many legs is that altogether?   _____ legs

2. Suzy took four cookies. If she ate half of the cookies, how many did she eat?   _____ cookies

3. Scott has 3 brothers and 2 sisters. How many children are in Scott's family?   _____ children

4. Alexis had 24 beads. She put 12 beads on a bracelet. How many beads does she have left?   _____ beads

©2005 by Evan-Moor Corp. • Daily Summer Activities 1-2 • EMC 1028

Geography

Name the oceans.

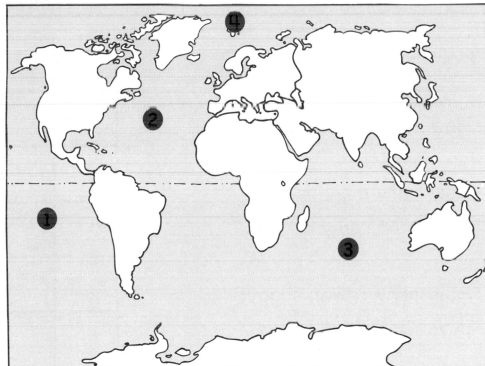

Word Box

Indian

Atlantic

Arctic

Pacific

1.

2.

3.

4.

On my birthday, I would like to _____

_____

_____

_____

1. How many rainy days? _____

2. How many cloudy days? _____

3. How many more sunny days than rainy days? _____

4. How many fewer foggy days than cloudy days? _____

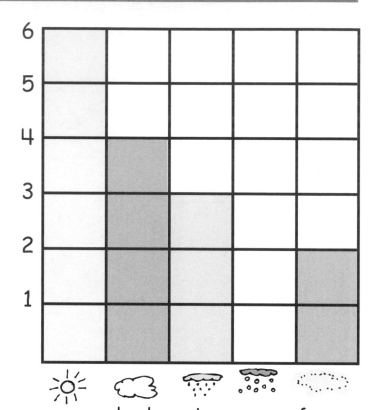

6					
5					
4					
3					
2					
1					

sunny cloudy rainy snowy foggy

Letters – Sounds – Words – Letters

Color the balloons.
Write the color words in alphabetical order.

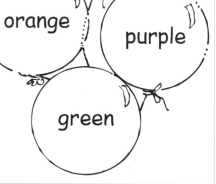

yellow
blue
red
orange
purple
green

1. _____   4. _____

2. _____   5. _____

3. _____   6. _____

©2005 by Evan-Moor Corp. • Daily Summer Activities 1-2 • EMC 1028

Read It! Read these words to an adult.

glad	plan	black	slip	flag	
glass	plant	block	slide	flip	
globe	plate	blanket	slap	flower	

grin	frog	drop	train	crack	
green	front	dress	track	crook	
grass	frost	drive	treat	crust	

I can read all of these words.   yes   no

MATH⊙TIME

Count the money in each purse.

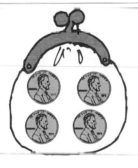

_____ ¢

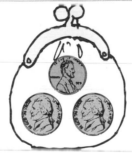

_____ ¢

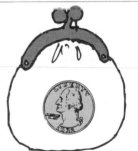

_____ ¢

_____ ¢

_____ ¢

_____ ¢

Friday   Week 10

Help Me!

This bird is lost. Her babies need food.
Help her get back to her nest.

Color the boxes to count by 5s.

5	10	15	20	28
16	23	19	32	25	29
50	45	40	35	30	46
55	27	43	84	77	22
60	52	80	85	90	95
65	70	75	94	88	100
68	43	96	52	74	

©2005 by Evan-Moor Corp. • Daily Summer Activities 1-2 • EMC 1028

Answer Key

Checking your child's work is an important part of learning. It allows you to see what your child knows well and what areas need more practice. It also provides an opportunity for you to help your child understand that making mistakes is a part of learning.

When an error is discovered, ask your child to look carefully at the question or problem. Errors often occur through misreading the problem. Your child can quickly correct these errors.

The answer key pages can be used in several ways:

- Remove the answer pages and give the book to your child. Go over the answers with him or her as each day's work is completed.

- Leave the answer pages in the book and give the practice pages to your child one day at a time.

- Leave the answer pages in the book so your child can check his or her own answers as the pages are completed. It is still important that you review the pages with your child if you use this method.

Page 11

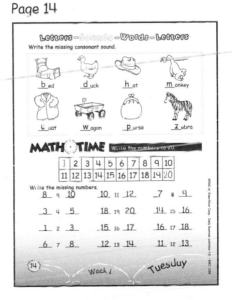

Page 12

Page 13

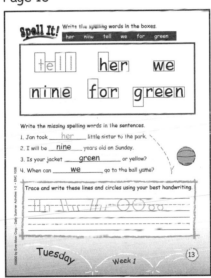

Page 14

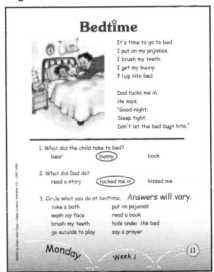

Page 15

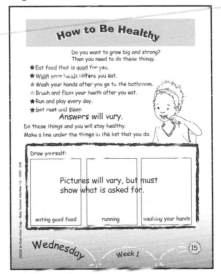

Page 16

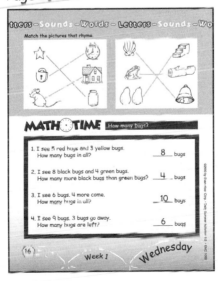

Page 17

Finding My Way Around

1. Start at the ⭐. Go left. What do you see?
2. Start at the ⭐. Go down. What do you see?
3. Start at the ⭐. Go right. What do you see?

up / left / right / down

In My Own Words

Draw a snail in a garden.

Tell what the snail is doing.

Answers will vary.

Thursday — Week 1 — 17

Page 18

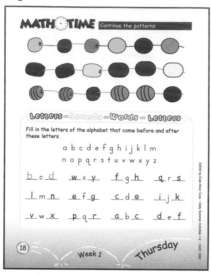

Thursday — Week 1 — 18

Page 19

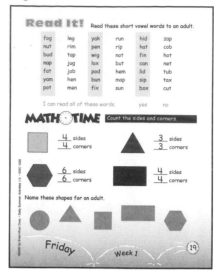

Friday — Week 1 — 19

Page 20

Week 1 — Friday — 20

Page 23

Monday — Week 2 — 23

Page 24

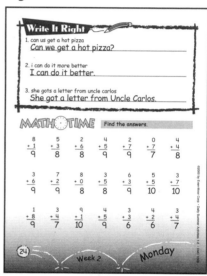

Monday — Week 2 — 24

Page 25

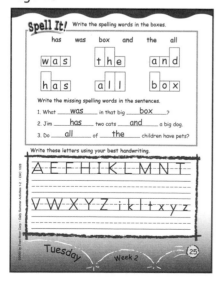

Tuesday — Week 2 — 25

Page 26

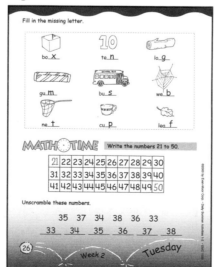

Week 2 — Tuesday — 26

Page 27

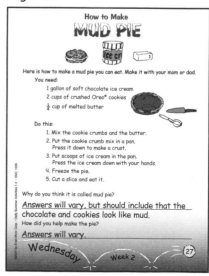

Wednesday — Week 2 — 27

Page 28

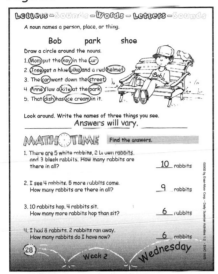

Page 29

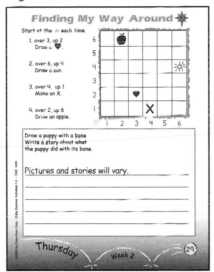

Page 30

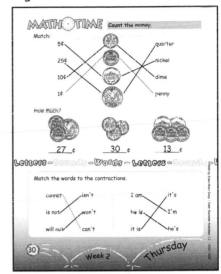

Page 31

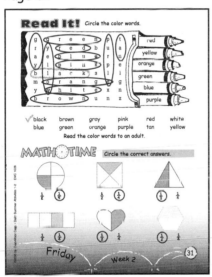

Page 32

Page 35

Page 36

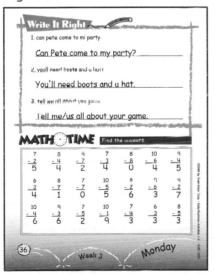

Page 37

Page 38

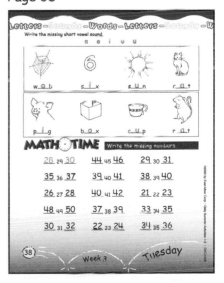

Page 39

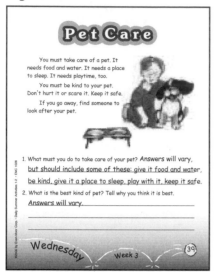

Pet Care

You must take care of a pet. It needs food and water. It needs a place to sleep. It needs playtime, too.

You must be kind to your pet. Don't hurt it or scare it. Keep it safe. If you go away, find someone to look after your pet.

1. What must you do to take care of your pet? *Answers will vary, but should include some of these: give it food and water, be kind, give it a place to sleep, play with it, keep it safe.*

2. What is the best kind of pet? Tell why you think it is best.
Answers will vary.

Wednesday   Week 3   39

Page 40

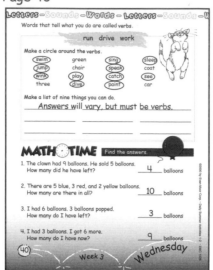

Letters - Sounds - Words - Letters - Sounds - L

Words that tell what you do are called verbs.

run drive work

Make a circle around the verbs.

(swim) green (sing) (sleep)
(jump) chair (speak) coat
(wink) (play) (catch) (see)
three (dive) (paint) car

Make a list of nine things you can do.

Answers will vary, but must be verbs.

MATH TIME Find the answers.

1. The clown had 9 balloons. He sold 5 balloons. How many did he have left? **4** balloons

2. There are 5 blue, 3 red, and 2 yellow balloons. How many are there in all? **10** balloons

3. I had 6 balloons. 3 balloons popped. How many do I have left? **3** balloons

4. I had 3 balloons. I got 6 more. How many do I have now? **9** balloons

40   Week 3   Wednesday

Page 41

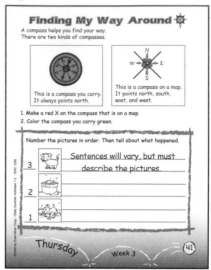

Finding My Way Around

A compass helps you find your way. There are two kinds of compasses.

This is a compass you carry. It always points north.

This is a compass on a map. It points north, south, east, and west.

1. Make a red X on the compass that is on a map.
2. Color the compass you carry green.

Number the pictures in order. Then tell about what happened.

3 *Sentences will vary, but must describe the pictures.*
2
1

Thursday   Week 3   41

Page 42

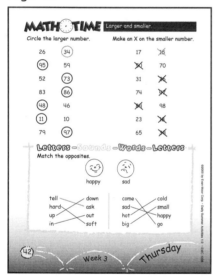

MATH TIME Larger and smaller.

Circle the larger number.   Make an X on the smaller number.

26 (34)   17 ✗16
(95) 59   ✗ 70
52 (73)   31 ✗
83 (86)   74 ✗
(48) 46   ✗ 98
(11) 10   23 ✗
79 (97)   65 ✗

Letters - Sounds - Words - Letters

Match the opposites.

happy   sad

tell — down   come — cold
hard — ask   sad — small
up — out   hot — happy
in — soft   big — go

42   Week 3   Thursday

Page 43

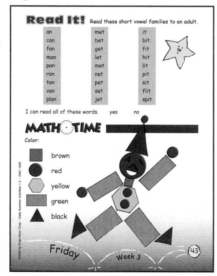

Read It! Read these short vowel families to an adult.

an	met	it
can	bet	bit
fan	get	fit
man	let	hit
pan	met	lit
ran	net	pit
tan	pet	sit
van	set	flit
plan	jet	spit

I can read all of these words.   yes   no

MATH TIME

Color:

brown
red
yellow
green
black

Friday   Week 3   43

Page 44

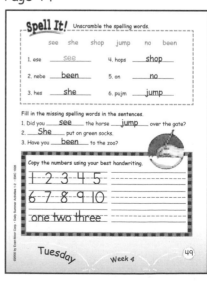

Look! Look!

Color the numbers hiding in this picture.

44   Week 3   Friday

Page 47

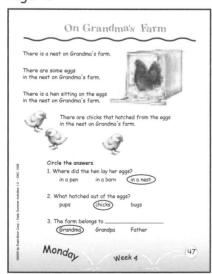

On Grandma's Farm

There is a nest on Grandma's farm.

There are some eggs in the nest on Grandma's farm.

There is a hen sitting on the eggs in the nest on Grandma's farm.

There are chicks that hatched from the eggs in the nest on Grandma's farm.

Circle the answers.
1. Where did the hen lay her eggs?
   in a pen   in a barn   (in a nest)

2. What hatched out of the eggs?
   pups   (chicks)   bugs

3. The farm belongs to
   (Grandma)   Grandpa   Father

Monday   Week 4   47

Page 48

Write It Right

1. hes the biggest boy i ever seen
He's the biggest boy I ever saw. or
He is the biggest boy I have ever seen.

2. max and me cant buy no popcorn
Max and I can't buy any popcorn.

3. we goes to the park every sunday
We go to the park every Sunday.

MATH TIME Find the answers.

1	3	1	3	6	4	8
+8	+7	+2	+6	+5	+1	+2
9	9	10	9	9	8	10

2	3	5	5	5	7	2
+5	+4	+2	+2	+1	+0	+6
9	10	10	9	8	9	9

48   Week 4   Monday

Page 49

Spell It! Unscramble the spelling words.

see she shop jump no been

1. ese **see**   4. hops **shop**
2. nebe **been**   5. on **no**
3. hes **she**   6. pujm **jump**

Fill in the missing spelling words in the sentences.
1. Did you **see** the horse **jump** over the gate?
2. **She** put on green socks.
3. Have you **been** to the zoo?

Copy the numbers using your best handwriting.
1 2 3 4 5
6 7 8 9 10
one two three

Tuesday   Week 4   49

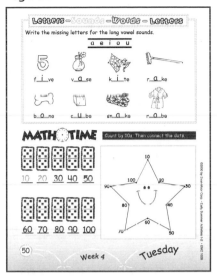

Letters – Sounds – Words – Letters

Write the missing letters for the long vowel sounds.

a e i o u

f i ve   v a se   k i te   r a ke

b o ne   c u be   sn a ke   r o be

MATH TIME — Count by 10s. Then connect the dots.

10 20 30 40 50
60 70 80 90 100

50   Week 4   Tuesday

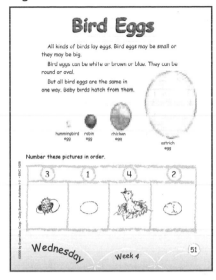

Bird Eggs

All kinds of birds lay eggs. Bird eggs may be small or they may be big.

Bird eggs can be white or brown or blue. They can be round or oval.

But all bird eggs are the same in one way. Baby birds hatch from them.

hummingbird egg   robin egg   chicken egg   ostrich egg

Number these pictures in order.

3   1   4   2

Wednesday   Week 4   51

Letters – Sounds – Words – Letters – Sounds

Write each set of words in alphabetical order.

a b c d e f g h i j k l m
n o p q r s t u v w x y z

box — apple
apple — box
can — can

elephant — duck
duck — elephant
fox — fox

mice — chair
chair — mice
zoo — zoo

three — blue
six — six
blue — three

MATH TIME — Figure out how much fruit.

1. I saw 10 bananas in a bunch. 6 of the bananas were yellow. How many were still green?   4 bananas

2. I have 5 oranges. I need 8 oranges. How many more do I need?   3 oranges

3. I found 9 apples. 3 apples were red. 2 apples were green. How many apples were yellow?   4 apples

4. I picked 6 pears yesterday. I picked 4 pears today. How many pears did I pick in all?   10 pears

52   Week 4   Wednesday

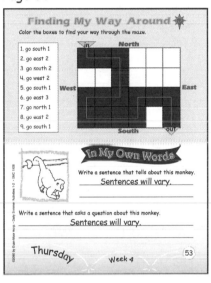

Finding My Way Around

Color the boxes to find your way through the maze.

1. go south 1
2. go east 2
3. go south 2
4. go west 2
5. go south 1
6. go east 3
7. go north 1
8. go east 1
9. go south 1

North   West   East   South

In My Own Words

Write a sentence that tells about this monkey.
Sentences will vary.

Write a sentence that asks a question about this monkey.
Sentences will vary.

Thursday   Week 4   53

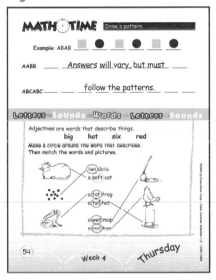

MATH TIME — Draw a pattern.

Example: ABAB

AABB   Answers will vary, but must

ABCABC   follow the patterns.

Letters – Sounds – Words – Letters – Sounds

Adjectives are words that describe things.

big   hot   six   red

Make a circle around the word that describes. Then match the words and pictures.

ten dots
a soft cat
a fat frog
a tall hat
a wet mop
a red hen

54   Week 4   Thursday

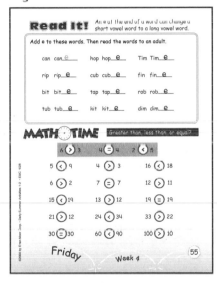

Read It! — An e at the end of a word can change a short vowel word to a long vowel word.

Add e to these words. Then read the words to an adult.

can cane   hop hope   Tim Time
rip ripe   cub cube   fin fine
bit bite   tap tape   rob robe
tub tube   kit kite   dim dime

MATH TIME — Greater than, less than, or equal?

6 > 3	4 = 4	2 < 5
5 < 9	4 < 9	16 < 18
6 > 2	7 = 7	12 < 11
15 < 19	13 > 12	19 = 19
21 > 12	24 < 34	33 > 22
30 = 30	60 < 90	100 > 10

Friday   Week 4   55

ANIMAL Crossword Puzzle

Across
1. frog
4. hen
6. whale
8. pig
9. cow

Down
2.
3.
5. walrus
7. goat
10. mice

Word Box

cow   goat   hen   pig   walrus
frog   goose   mice   sheep   whale

56   Week 4   Friday

Lady AND Bubbles

Matt has two dogs. One is a big yellow dog. Her name is Lady. One dog is a frisky puppy. Her name is Bubbles.

Bubbles likes to play with Lady. Sometimes Lady gets tired of Bubbles. She growls and moves away. Bubbles will try to play with Lady again. Then Matt takes Bubbles to the front yard. At last Lady can get some rest.

1. Which dog is the biggest?
Bubbles   (Lady)

2. What does Bubbles like to do?
play with a ball   (play with Lady)   take a nap

3. How does Lady show she is tired of playing?
(growls)   smiles   sleeps

4. Why does Matt put Bubbles in the front yard?
to play with Bubbles   (to let Lady rest)

Monday   Week 5   59

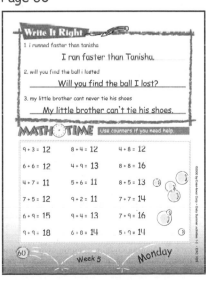

Write It Right

1. i runned faster than tanisha
I ran faster than Tanisha.

2. will you find the ball i losted
Will you find the ball I lost?

3. my little brother cant never tie his shoes
My little brother can't tie his shoes.

MATH TIME — Use counters if you need help.

9 + 3 = 12	8 + 4 = 12	4 + 8 = 12
6 + 6 = 12	4 + 9 = 13	8 + 8 = 16
4 + 7 = 11	5 + 6 = 11	8 + 5 = 13
7 + 5 = 12	9 + 2 = 11	7 + 7 = 14
6 + 9 = 15	9 + 4 = 13	7 + 9 = 16
9 + 9 = 18	6 + 8 = 14	5 + 9 = 14

60   Week 5   Monday

Page 61

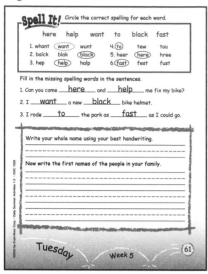

Spell It! Circle the correct spelling for each word.

here help want to black fast

1. whant (want) wunt
2. balck blak (black)
3. hep (help) halp
4. (to) tew tou
5. heer (here) hree
6. (fast) fest fust

Fill in the missing spelling words in the sentences.
1. Can you come __here__ and __help__ me fix my bike?
2. I __want__ a new __black__ bike helmet.
3. I rode __to__ the park as __fast__ as I could go.

Write your whole name using your best handwriting.

Now write the first names of the people in your family.

Tuesday Week 5 61

Page 62

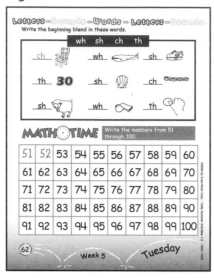

Letters – Sounds – Words – Letters – Sounds
Write the beginning blend in these words.

wh sh ch th

ch ___ wh ___ sh ___
th __30__ sh ___ ch ___
sh ___ wh ___ th ___

MATH TIME Write the numbers from 51 through 100.

51	52	53	54	55	56	57	58	59	60
61	62	63	64	65	66	67	68	69	70
71	72	73	74	75	76	77	78	79	80
81	82	83	84	85	86	87	88	89	90
91	92	93	94	95	96	97	98	99	100

62 Week 5 Tuesday

Page 63

Dogs

There are many kinds of dogs. There are big dogs and small dogs. There are long dogs and short dogs.

Some dogs have ears that stand up. Some dogs have ears that hang down.

There are dogs with long tails, short tails, and no tails.

Dog hair can be long or short. There is even one dog with no hair! Dog hair can be one color. It can be more than one color.

Tell what each dog looks like.

Answers will vary, but could include words describing size, color, ear shape, tail length, etc.

Wednesday Week 5 63

Page 64

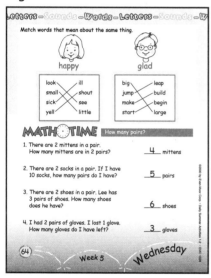

Letters – Sounds – Words – Letters – Sounds – W
Match words that mean about the same thing.

happy   glad

look — ill
small — shout
sick — see
yell — little

big — leap
jump — build
make — begin
start — large

MATH TIME How many pairs?

1. There are 2 mittens in a pair. How many mittens are in 2 pairs? __4__ mittens
2. There are 2 socks in a pair. If I have 10 socks, how many pairs do I have? __5__ pairs
3. There are 2 shoes in a pair. Lee has 3 pairs of shoes. How many shoes does he have? __6__ shoes
4. I had 2 pairs of gloves. I lost 1 glove. How many gloves do I have left? __3__ gloves

64 Week 5 Wednesday

Page 65

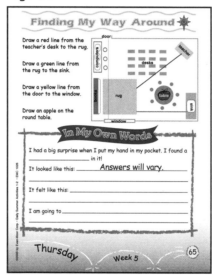

Finding My Way Around

Draw a red line from the teacher's desk to the rug.

Draw a green line from the rug to the sink.

Draw a yellow line from the door to the window.

Draw an apple on the round table.

In My Own Words

I had a big surprise when I put my hand in my pocket. I found a ___ in it!
It looked like this: __Answers will vary.__
It felt like this: ___
I am going to ___

Thursday Week 5 65

Page 66

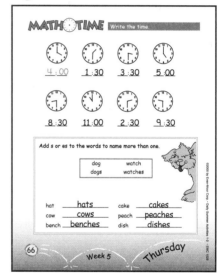

MATH TIME Write the time.

4:00 1:30 3:30 5:00
8:30 11:00 2:30 9:30

Add s or es to the words to name more than one.

| dog | watch |
| dogs | watches |

hat __hats__   cake __cakes__
cow __cows__   peach __peaches__
bench __benches__   dish __dishes__

66 Week 5 Thursday

Page 67

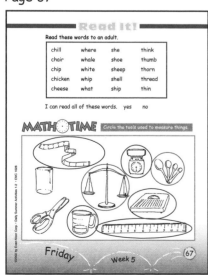

Read It!

Read these words to an adult.

chill	where	she	think
chair	whale	shoe	thumb
chip	white	sheep	thorn
chicken	whip	shell	thread
cheese	what	ship	thin

I can read all of these words.   yes   no

MATH TIME Circle the tools used to measure things.

Friday Week 5 67

Page 68

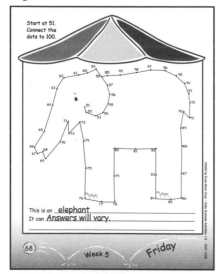

Start at 51. Connect the dots to 100.

This is an __elephant__
It can __Answers will vary.__

68 Week 5 Friday

Page 71

Tim's Lost Lizard

Tim went to feed his lizard. "Oh, no!" yelled Tim. "My lizard is gone!"

Tim ran to the backyard to find his sister. "My lizard got out of its cage. Can you help me find it?" asked Tim.

Tim and his sister looked under Tim's bed. They looked in Tim's closet. They looked in Tim's toy box. They did not find the lizard. Tim was so sad.

Just then Tim's sister saw something. She went to the window. There was the lizard sitting in the sun. Tim picked up his pet. Tim was happy now.

Circle the answers.
1. Why was Tim sad?
   His ball was lost.
   (His lizard was gone.)
2. Where didn't Tim and his sister look for the lizard?
   under the bed
   (in the backyard)
   in the closet
   in the toy box
3. Where was the lizard?
   (by the window)
   on the desk
4. Why do you think the lizard was sitting in the sun?
   to look for a fly to eat
   (to get warm)

Monday Week 6 71

©2005 by Evan-Moor Corp. • Daily Summer Activities 1-2 • EMC 1028

Page 72

Write It Right

1. will you pushing she in the swing
   Will you push her in the swing?

2. he gots lots of candy
   He has lots of candy.

3. maurice taked his byke to school
   Maurice took his bike to school.

MATH TIME — Use counters if you need help.

11 −3 = 8	15 −6 = 9	12 −4 = 8	18 −9 = 9	14 −7 = 7	10 −8 = 2
16 −8 = 8	13 −7 = 6	17 −9 = 8	11 −5 = 6	16 −9 = 7	12 −7 = 5
13 −4 = 9	15 −8 = 7	12 −8 = 4	14 −9 = 5	17 −8 = 9	12 −6 = 6

(72) Week 6 Monday

Page 73

Spell It! Circle the correct spelling for each word.

small yellow letter little
happy silly messy hill

1. smal (small) slam
2. (happy) hapy happe
3. letor lettre (letter)
4. (messy) mesy meesy
5. yelllow (yellow) yello
6. sille (silly) sily
7. hil (hill) hll
8. (little) litlle litul

Copy the names of the school days using your best handwriting.

Monday
Tuesday
Wednesday
Thursday
Friday

Tuesday Week 6 (73)

Page 74

Letters – Sounds – Words – Letters

Fill in the missing letters oa ee

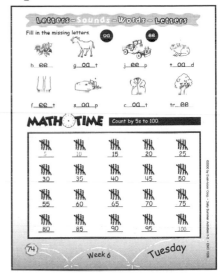

b ee g oa t j ee p t oa d
r ee t s oa p c oa t tr ee

MATH TIME — Count by 5s to 100.

5	10	15	20	25
30	35	40	45	50
55	60	65	70	75
80	85	90	95	100

(74) Week 6 Tuesday

Page 75

Lizards

Lizards have scales on their skin. They have four legs. Their feet have long toes. Most lizards have long tails.

Lizards eat insects, spiders, and worms.

Lizards can run and climb.

Most lizards lay eggs. Mother lizards hide their eggs in sand or soft dirt. Lizard babies can run and find food as soon as they hatch.

Color the lizards.

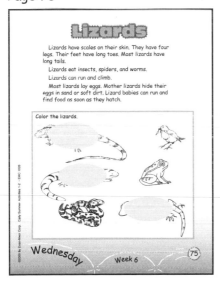

Wednesday Week 6 (75)

Page 76

Letters – Sounds – Words – Letters – Sounds – L

Write rhyming words in the sentences.

1. Jack and __Jill__
   went up the __hill__

2. Little Bo __Peep__
   has lost her __sheep__

3. Little Miss __Muffet__
   sat on a __tuffet__

4. Hickory, dickory, __dock__
   the mouse ran up the __clock__

Word Box
Peep
hill
Muffet
sheep
clock
tuffet
Jill
dock

MATH TIME — Find the answers.

1. 10 kites went up in the air. 7 kites fell down.
   How many kites are still in the air? __3__ kites

2. 3 boys, 4 girls, and 1 teacher played a game.
   How many played the game? __8__ players

3. Will made 6 baskets and Mark made 4 baskets.
   How many baskets did they make in all? __10__ baskets

4. 4 children want to swing. There are 4 swings.
   How many children have to wait for a turn? __5__ children

(76) Week 6 Wednesday

Page 77

Finding My Way Around

This is Earth.
It is the planet we live on.

Color the land green.
Color the water blue.

In My Own Words

Write a letter to a friend. Tell your friend about something you did today.

Dear _____

Letters will vary.

Your friend,

_____

Thursday Week 6 (77)

Page 78

MATH TIME — How long are the lizards?

__4__ inches

__3__ inches

Letters – Sounds – Words – Letters

Pronouns are words that take the place of nouns.

He she We it
They them Her us

Write a pronoun on each line.

1. Dad has a box. __He__ puts tools in __it__

2. Mrs. Lee went to the store. __Her__ son went to the store, too.

3. Stan and Will like to play ball. __They__ like to play ball.

4. Peter has a soccer ball. __He__ plays with __it__

5. Ann and I are going to school. __We__ are going to school.

(78) Week 6 Thursday

Page 79

Read It! Read these words to an adult.

the	a	A	for
they	from	of	to
you	with	I	this
that	was	are	have
by	all	how	said
were	as	your	or
The	want	draw	circle

I can read all of these words. yes ☐ no ☐

MATH TIME — How many 10s and 1s?

29 = __2__ tens and __9__ ones   10 10
22 = __2__ tens and __2__ ones   10 10
37 = __3__ tens and __7__ ones   10 10 10
46 = __4__ tens and __6__ ones   10 10 10 10

Friday Week 6 (79)

Page 80

A Number Word

Crossword Puzzle

Name the numbers.

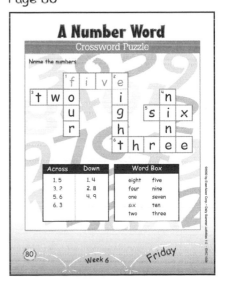

1. f i v e
3. t w o
   u
   r
   i
   g
   h
   t
5. s i x
6. t h r e e
4. n i n e

Across	Down	Word Box	
1. 5	1. 4	eight	five
3. 2	2. 8	four	nine
5. 6	4. 9	one	seven
6. 3		six	ten
		two	three

(80) Week 6 Friday

Page 83

A Lost Tooth

"Look! My tooth came out!" shouted Rosa. "I'm going to put it under my pillow. I hope the tooth fairy will come."

Rosa's teacher put the tooth in a small box. Rosa put the box in her pocket.

After school Rosa ran to meet her sister. "My tooth fell out," she said. Rosa put a hand in her pocket to get the box. It was gone. She began to cry.

Just then Jorge ran up. "You dropped this box," he said.

Rosa was so happy. She gave Jorge a big hug. "I will keep it in my hand," she said. "I don't want to drop it again."

1. What was Rosa going to do with her tooth?
   put it under her pillow
2. Why did the teacher put the tooth in a little box?
   so Rosa would not lose it
3. Who found Rosa's tooth?
   Jorge
4. How many teeth have you lost?
   Answers will vary.

Monday — Week 7 — (83)

Page 84

Write It Right

1. dad and me goed fishing friday
   Dad and I went fishing Friday.
2. ellie hitted her head when she falled
   Ellie hit her head when she fell.
3. i found dads note in my lunch box
   I found Dad's note in my lunch box.

MATH TIME — Find the answers.

62 +36 98	71 +18 89	82 +15 97	93 +3 96	25 +24 49
45 +52 97	61 +37 98	17 +82 99	97 +2 99	48 +51 99
23 +12 35	45 +34 79	32 +56 88	81 +17 98	22 +33 55

(84) — Week 7 — Monday

Page 85

Spell It! Unscramble the spelling words.

most   find   gave
next   have   went

1. dinf — find
2. xetn — next
3. toms — most
4. twen — went
5. vage — gave
6. heav — have

Write a sentence using each of these spelling words.   going   doing
1. Sentences will vary.
2. _____

Copy this poem using your best handwriting.

Rain, rain, go away,
Come again another day.

Tuesday — Week 7 — (85)

Page 86

Letters — Sounds — Words — Letters

Fill in the missing letters.   ai   ay

p_ai_nt   tr_ai_n   h_ay_   j_ay_

r_ai_n   cl_ay_   ch_ai_n   tr_ay_

Circle the words with the sound of a in say.
1. The hay is in the box.
2. The man spilled his paint.
3. It has started to rain.
4. Mother has a gray coat.

MATH TIME — Fill in the missing numbers.

51 52 53	63 64 65	89 90 91
67 68 69	86 87 88	61 62 63
79 80 81	76 77 78	80 81 82
98 99 100	68 69 70	55 56 57

(86) — Week 7 — Tuesday

Page 87

Teeth

When you are grown you will have 28 to 32 teeth in all.

You need your teeth when you eat. Teeth tear and grind your food into small bits. Then you can swallow the food.

You must take care of your teeth. Brush and floss your teeth every day. Go to the dentist, too. Then you will have strong teeth.

1. How do teeth help you eat?
   tear and grind food into small bits so you can swallow it

2. What can you do to make your teeth strong?
   brush, floss, and go to the dentist

Wednesday — Week 7 — (87)

Page 88

Letters — Sounds — Words — Letters — Sounds —

berry   berries

Drop the y and add ies to name more than one.
1. city — cities
2. pony — ponies
3. baby — babies
4. fairy — fairies
5. cherry — cherries
6. fly — flies

Some words change to show more than one.
1. man — men
2. mouse — mice
3. tooth — teeth
4. foot — feet

MATH TIME — Find the answers.

1. Ali took 10 cookies from the bag. He gave 2 cookies to Marta. He ate 3 cookies. How many cookies are left? — 5 cookies

2. A frog ate 12 bugs. A toad ate 15 bugs. How many bugs did they eat in all? — 27 bugs

3. I gave my puppy six bones. He ate three bones. How many bones are left? — 3 bones

4. It is 5 o'clock. We are going to eat supper in 1 hour. At what time will we eat? — 6 o'clock

(88) — Week 7 — Wednesday

Page 89

Geography

This is a globe.
It is round like Earth.
We use a globe to find places.

Color the land green.
Color the water blue.

In My Own Words

Write a sentence that tells about this clown.
Sentences will vary.

Write a sentence that asks a question about this clown.
Sentences will vary.

Thursday — Week 7 — (89)

Page 90

MATH TIME   Color the fractions.

Color ½   Color ¼
Color ¼   Color ½

Letters — Sounds — Words — Letters
Circle who is talking.
Underline what is being said.

Lee said, "I'll get us something to drink."

1. "Do you have a pet dog?" asked Mark.
2. Sum shouted, "Keep away from that fire!"
3. "Why do I have to go to bed now?" asked Raul.
4. Will said, "I like to play ball with my friends."
5. Mike asked, "How soon will it be dinnertime?"

(90) — Week 7 — Thursday

Page 91

Read It!   Write the missing letters.
Read the words to an adult.

ee	oa	ai	ay
b_ee_	c_oa_t	r_ai_n	s_ay_
tr_ee_	g_oa_t	g_ai_n	w_ay_
s_ee_n	cr_oa_k	p_ai_l	pl_ay_
thr_ee_	fl_oa_t	w_ai_t	cl_ay_
str_ee_t	c_oa_ch	p_ai_nt	st_ay_

MATH TIME   Find and mark the shapes.

sphere   cone   cube

Friday — Week 7 — (91)

Page 92

Good to Eat

I'm hard as a rock when I go into the pot.
I'm fluffy and white when I get very hot.

What am I? **popcorn**

Draw and color the other side of the picture.

92 • Week 7 • Friday

Page 95

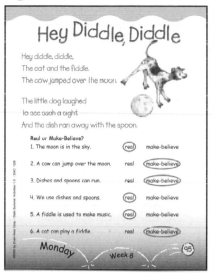

Hey Diddle, Diddle

Hey diddle, diddle,
The cat and the fiddle.
The cow jumped over the moon.

The little dog laughed
To see such a sight
And the dish ran away with the spoon.

Real or Make-Believe?
1. The moon is in the sky. (real) make-believe
2. A cow can jump over the moon. real (make-believe)
3. Dishes and spoons can run. real (make-believe)
4. We use dishes and spoons. (real) make-believe
5. A fiddle is used to make music. (real) make-believe
6. A cat can play a fiddle. real (make-believe)

Monday • Week 8 • 95

Page 96

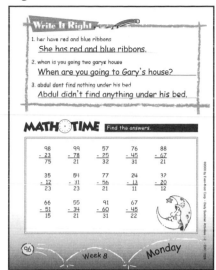

Write It Right

1. her have red and blue ribbons
She has red and blue ribbons.

2. when is you going two garys house
When are you going to Gary's house?

3. abdul dont find nothing under his bed
Abdul didn't find anything under his bed.

MATH TIME Find the answers.

98 − 23 = 75	99 − 78 = 21	57 − 25 = 32	76 − 45 = 31	88 − 67 = 21
35 − 12 = 23	54 − 31 = 23	77 − 56 = 21	24 − 13 = 11	32 − 20 = 12
66 − 51 = 15	55 − 34 = 21	91 − 60 = 31	67 − 45 = 22	

96 • Week 8 • Monday

Page 97

Spell It! Find these spelling words in the word search.

zoo   some   sitting   home
funny   running   clown   brown

b	c	l	o	w	n	q	s
r	u	n	n	i	n	g	o
o	z	f	u	n	n	y	m
w	o	x	h	o	m	e	e
n	o	o	m	e	z	s	i
s	i	t	t	i	n	g	n

Write the two spelling words that rhyme.
brown   **clown**

Write your address using your best handwriting.

_____
house number and street name
_____
city   state   zip

Tuesday • Week 8 • 97

Page 98

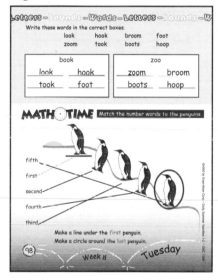

Letters – Sounds – Words – Letters – Sounds – W

Write these words in the correct boxes.
look   hook   broom   foot
zoom   took   boots   hoop

book	
look	hook
took	foot

zoo	
zoom	broom
boots	hoop

MATH TIME Match the number words to the penguins.

fifth
first
second
fourth
third

Make a line under the first penguin.
Make a circle around the last penguin.

98 • Week 8 • Tuesday

Page 99

Run, Swim, Fly

Do you ever watch animals move? If you do, you will see them move in many ways.

Animals on land may walk, run, jump, or hop. Some, like snakes or snails, crawl.

Bats and most birds fly. Insects like bees and ladybugs fly, too.

Fish and whales live in the water. Most animals that live in water swim.

Circle yes or no.
1. All animals move in the same ways. yes (no)
2. Bats can fly. (yes) no
3. Some snakes can run. yes (no)
4. Fish swim in the water. (yes) no

Name one animal that can move in this way.
Answers will vary, but could include:
swim **fish**   crawl **snake**   fly **bird**

List ways you can move.
Answers will vary.

Wednesday • Week 8 • 99

Page 100

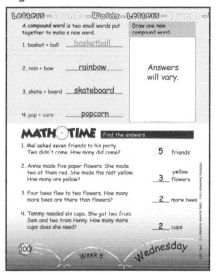

Letters – Sounds – Words – Letters – Sounds –

A compound word is two small words put together to make a new word.

1. basket + ball   **basketball**
2. rain + bow   **rainbow**
3. skate + board   **skateboard**
4. pop + corn   **popcorn**

Draw one new compound word.
Answers will vary.

MATH TIME Find the answers.

1. Mel asked seven friends to his party. Two didn't come. How many did come? **5** friends
2. Annie made five paper flowers. She made two of them red. She made the rest yellow. How many are yellow? **3** yellow flowers
3. Four bees flew to two flowers. How many more bees are there than flowers? **2** more bees
4. Tammy needed six cups. She got two from Sam and two from Penny. How many more cups does she need? **2** cups

100 • Week 8 • Wednesday

Page 101

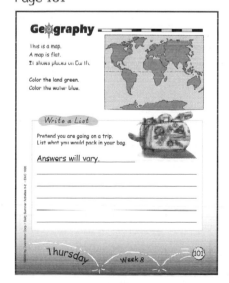

Geography

This is a map.
A map is flat.
It shows places on Earth.

Color the land green.
Color the water blue.

Write a List

Pretend you are going on a trip.
List what you would pack in your bag.

Answers will vary.
_____
_____
_____

Thursday • Week 8 • 101

Page 102

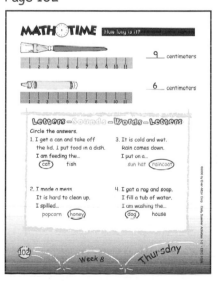

MATH TIME How long is it?

9 centimeters

6 centimeters

Letters – Sounds – Words – Letters

Circle the answers.

1. I get a can and take off the lid. I put food in a dish. I am feeding the...
(cat) fish

2. I made a mess. It is hard to clean up. I spilled...
popcorn (honey)

3. It is cold and wet. Rain comes down. I put on a...
sun hat (raincoat)

4. I got a rag and soap. I fill a tub of water. I am washing the...
(dog) house

102 • Week 8 • Thursday

Page 103

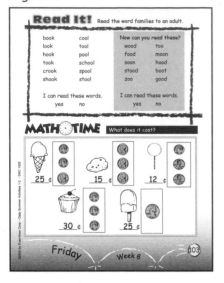

Read It! Read the word families to an adult.

book	cool	Now can you read these?	
look	tool	wood	too
hook	pool	food	moon
took	school	soon	hood
crook	spool	stood	boot
shook	stool	zoo	good

I can read these words. yes no

I can read these words. yes no

MATH TIME What does it cost?

25 ¢   15   12 ¢

30 ¢   25 ¢

Friday   Week 8   103

Page 104

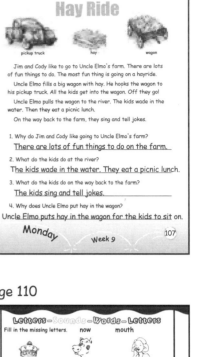

The Cowboy
Draw and color the other side.

104   Week 8   Friday

Page 107

Hay Ride

pickup truck   hay   wagon

Jim and Cody like to go to Uncle Elmo's farm. There are lots of fun things to do. The most fun thing is going on a hayride.

Uncle Elmo fills a big wagon with hay. He hooks the wagon to his pickup truck. All the kids get into the wagon. Off they go!

Uncle Elmo pulls the wagon to the river. The kids wade in the water. Then they eat a picnic lunch.

On the way back to the farm, they sing and tell jokes.

1. Why do Jim and Cody like going to Uncle Elmo's farm?
There are lots of fun things to do on the farm.

2. What do the kids do at the river?
The kids wade in the water. They eat a picnic lunch.

3. What do the kids do on the way back to the farm?
The kids sing and tell jokes.

4. Why does Uncle Elmo put hay in the wagon?
Uncle Elmo puts hay in the wagon for the kids to sit on.

Monday   Week 9   107

Page 108

Write It Right

1. sally hided the box inn the closet
Sally hid the box in the closet.

2. hes the most tall boy in our class
He's the tallest boy in our class.

3. torys more faster than we is
Tory's faster than we are.

MATH TIME Find the answers.

23	22	68	27	91
+ 34	+ 46	- 42	+ 72	- 71
57	68	26	99	20

55	54	73	99	28
- 34	+ 25	+ 16	- 83	+ 71
21	79	89	16	99

39	59	52	42	98
- 3	- 36	+ 42	+ 32	- 26
36	23	94	74	72

108   Week 9   Monday

Page 109

Spell It! Unscramble the spelling words.

make	two	smile	like
making	use	smiling	sleep

1. wot two
2. sue use
3. kame make
4. miles smile
5. peels sleep
6. keil like

Write sentences using making and smiling.
1. Sentences will vary.
2.

Copy these words using your best handwriting.

Queen's quilt

Frog's fat flies

Zeke's zipper

Tuesday   Week 9   109

Page 110

Letters – Sounds – Words – Letters
Fill in the missing letters. now mouth

cr OW n   c OW   sh OU t

h OU se   cl OW n   m OU se

MATH TIME Count by 2s to 20.

2   4   6   8   10
12   14   16   18   20

Connect the dots.

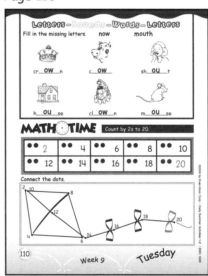

110   Week 9   Tuesday

Page 111

A Pickup Truck

People use pickup trucks when they work. A farmer hauls hay, feed, and animals. A carpenter hauls tools and lumber. A gardener hauls large and small plants.

A family may use a pickup truck when they move. The pickup can haul furniture and boxes to their new home.

People use a pickup truck for fun, too. They may use a pickup when they go camping. Horse owners may use a pickup truck to pull their horse trailers.

For work or for play, a pickup can be useful.

Circle the correct words.

Who is using the pickup truck?

1. The pickup is loaded with tents and sleeping bags.
carpenter / farmer / (camper)

2. The pickup is loaded with plants, rakes, and shovels.
(gardener) / horse owner / carpenter

3. The pickup is loaded with lumber, ladders, and hammers.
farmer / (carpenter) / gardener

Wednesday   Week 9   111

Page 112

Letters – Sounds – Words – Letters – Sounds – W

An abbreviation is a short way to say something.

doctor–Dr.   quart–qt.

Match the word to its abbreviation.

Street	Dec.
December	cm
centimeter	St.

Mister	in.
inch	Mr.
Sunday	Sun.

MATH TIME How many?

1. Art made 6 stacks of blocks. He put 5 blocks in each stack. How many blocks did he use in all? 30 blocks

2. Joe walked 4 blocks to Ken's house. Then he walked back home. How many blocks did he walk in all? 8 blocks

3. Morris has 2 bikes and 1 wagon. How many wheels does he have on these toys? 8 wheels

4. Amy eats a banana every day. How many bananas does she eat in a week? 7 bananas

112   Week 9   Wednesday

Page 113

Geography

These pictures are used to show things on a map.

△ tree
⌂ mountain
ᔑ river

Color the rivers on the map blue.
Color the trees on the map green.
Make a brown X on the mountains on the map.

In My Own Words

Write a funny story about a dog in the circus.
Stories will vary.

Thursday   Week 9   113

©2005 by Evan-Moor Corp. • Daily Summer Activities 1-2 • EMC 1028

Page 114

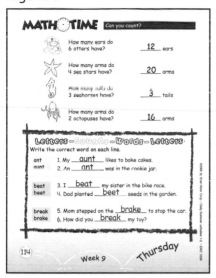

MATH TIME | Can you count?

How many ears do 6 otters have? __12__ ears

How many arms do 4 sea stars have? __20__ arms

How many tails do 3 seahorses have? __3__ tails

How many arms do 2 octopuses have? __16__ arms

Letters – Sounds – Words – Letters
Write the correct word on each line.

ant / aunt
1. My __aunt__ likes to bake cakes.
2. An __ant__ was in the cookie jar.

beat / beet
3. I __beat__ my sister in the bike race.
4. Dad planted __beet__ seeds in the garden.

break / brake
5. Mom stepped on the __brake__ to stop the car.
6. How did you __break__ my toy?

(114) Week 9 Thursday

Page 115

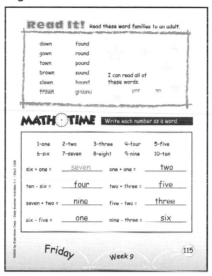

Read It! Read these word families to an adult.

down	found
gown	round
town	pound
brown	sound
clown	hound
frown	ground

I can read all of these words. yes no

MATH TIME | Write each number as a word.

| 1-one | 2-two | 3-three | 4-four | 5-five |
| 6-six | 7-seven | 8-eight | 9-nine | 10-ten |

six + one = __seven__   one + one = __two__

ten – six = __four__   two + three = __five__

seven + two = __nine__   five – two = __three__

six – five = __one__   nine – three = __six__

Friday Week 9 (115)

Page 116

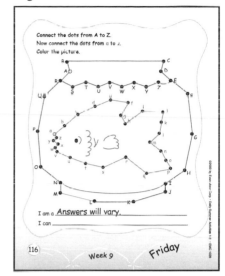

Connect the dots from A to Z.
Now connect the dots from a to z.
Color the picture.

I am a __Answers will vary.__
I can _____

(116) Week 9 Friday

Page 119

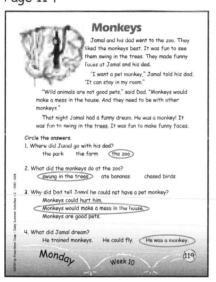

Monkeys

Jamal and his dad went to the zoo. They liked the monkeys best. It was fun to see them swing in the trees. They made funny faces at Jamal and his dad.

"I want a pet monkey," Jamal told his dad. "It can stay in my room."

"Wild animals are not good pets," said Dad. "Monkeys would make a mess in the house. And they need to be with other monkeys."

That night Jamal had a funny dream. He was a monkey! It was fun to swing in the trees. It was fun to make funny faces.

Circle the answers.
1. Where did Jamal go with his dad?
   the park   the farm   (the zoo)

2. What did the monkeys do at the zoo?
   (swung in the trees)   ate bananas   chased birds

3. Why did Dad tell Jamal he could not have a pet monkey?
   Monkeys could hurt him.
   (Monkeys would make a mess in the house.)
   Monkeys are good pets.

4. What did Jamal dream?
   He trained monkeys.   He could fly.   (He was a monkey.)

Monday Week 10 (119)

Page 120

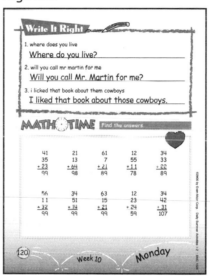

Write It Right
1. where does you live
   Where do you live?
2. will you call mr martin for me
   Will you call Mr. Martin for me?
3. i licked that book about them cowboys
   I liked that book about those cowboys.

MATH TIME | Find the answers.

41	21	61	12	34
35	13	7	55	33
+ 23	+ 64	+ 21	+ 11	+ 22
99	98	89	78	89

56	34	63	12	34
11	51	15	23	42
+ 32	+ 14	+ 21	+ 24	+ 31
99	99	99	59	107

(120) Week 10 Monday

Page 121

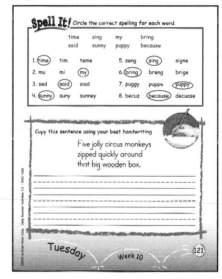

Spell It! Circle the correct spelling for each word.

time   sing   my   bring
said   sunny   puppy   because

1. (time)   tim   teme
2. mu   mi   (my)
3. sed   (said)   siad
4. (sunny)   suny   sunney
5. seng   (sing)   signe
6. (bring)   breng   brige
7. puggy   puppe   (puppy)
8. becuz   (because)   decuase

Copy this sentence using your best handwriting.

Five jolly circus monkeys zipped quickly around that big wooden box.

Tuesday Week 10 (121)

Page 122

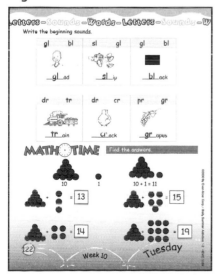

Letters – Sounds – Words – Letters – Sounds – W
Write the beginning sounds.

| gl bl | sl gl | gl bl |
| __gl__ ad | __sl__ ip | __bl__ ack |

| dr tr | dr cr | pr gr |
| __tr__ ain | __cr__ ack | __gr__ apes |

MATH TIME | Find the answers.

10   1   10 + 1 = 11

□ + □ = [13]   □ + □ = [15]

□ + □ = [14]   □ + □ = [19]

(122) Week 10 Tuesday

Page 123

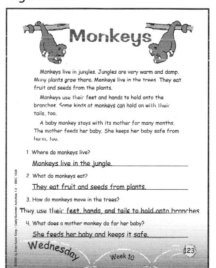

Monkeys

Monkeys live in jungles. Jungles are very warm and damp. Many plants grow there. Monkeys live in the trees. They eat fruit and seeds from the plants.

Monkeys use their feet and hands to hold onto the branches. Some kinds of monkeys can hold on with their tails, too.

A baby monkey stays with its mother for many months. The mother feeds her baby. She keeps her baby safe from harm, too.

1. Where do monkeys live?
   Monkeys live in the jungle.

2. What do monkeys eat?
   They eat fruit and seeds from plants.

3. How do monkeys move in the trees?
   They use their feet, hands, and tails to hold onto branches.

4. What does a mother monkey do for her baby?
   She feeds her baby and keeps it safe.

Wednesday Week 10 (123)

Page 124

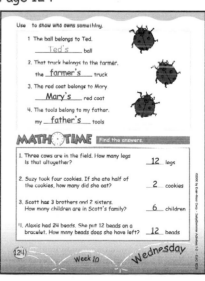

Use ' to show who owns something.

1. The ball belongs to Ted.
   __Ted's__ ball

2. That truck belongs to the farmer.
   the __farmer's__ truck

3. The red coat belongs to Mary.
   __Mary's__ red coat

4. The tools belong to my father.
   my __father's__ tools

MATH TIME | Find the answers.

1. Three cows are in the field. How many legs is that altogether? __12__ legs

2. Suzy took four cookies. If she ate half of the cookies, how many did she eat? __2__ cookies

3. Scott has 3 brothers and 2 sisters. How many children are in Scott's family? __6__ children

4. Alexis had 24 beads. She put 12 beads on a bracelet. How many beads does she have left? __12__ beads

(124) Week 10 Wednesday

Page 125

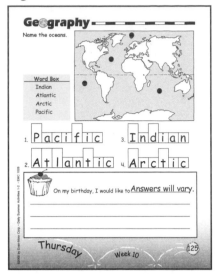

Geography

Name the oceans.

Word Box
Indian
Atlantic
Arctic
Pacific

1. Pacific   3. Indian
2. Atlantic   4. Arctic

On my birthday, I would like to Answers will vary.

Thursday   Week 10   125

Page 126

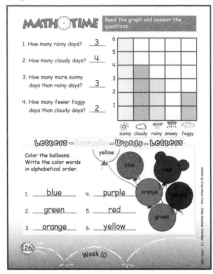

MATH TIME — Read the graph and answer the questions.

1. How many rainy days? 3
2. How many cloudy days? 4
3. How many more sunny days than rainy days? 3
4. How many fewer foggy days than cloudy days? 2

sunny cloudy rainy snowy foggy

Letters – Sounds – Words – Letters

Color the balloons.
Write the color words in alphabetical order.

yellow
blue
red
orange
purple
green

1. blue   4. purple
2. green   5. red
3. orange   6. yellow

126   Week 10

Page 127

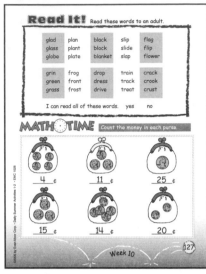

Read It! Read these words to an adult.

glad	plan	black	slip	flag
glass	plant	block	slide	flip
globe	plate	blanket	slap	flower

grin	frog	drop	train	crack
green	front	dress	track	crook
grass	frost	drive	treat	crust

I can read all of these words.   yes   no

MATH TIME   Count the money in each purse.

4 ¢   11 ¢   25 ¢

15 ¢   14 ¢   20 ¢

Week 10   127

Page 128

Help Me!

This bird is lost. Her babies need food.
Help her get back to her nest.

Color the boxes to count by 5s.

				28
16	23	19	32	29
				46
	27	43	84	77	22
	52			
			94	88
68	43	96	52	74

128   Week 10

Number Grid

1	2	3	4	5	6	7	8	9	10
11	12	13	14	15	16	17	18	19	20
21	22	23	24	25	26	27	28	29	30
31	32	33	34	35	36	37	38	39	40
41	42	43	44	45	46	47	48	49	50
51	52	53	54	55	56	57	58	59	60
61	62	63	64	65	66	67	68	69	70
71	72	73	74	75	76	77	78	79	80
81	82	83	84	85	86	87	88	89	90
91	92	93	94	95	96	97	98	99	100
101	102	103	104	105	106	107	108	109	110

Manuscript Writing

Aa Bb Cc Dd

Ee Ff Gg Hh

Ii Jj Kk Ll

Mm Nn Oo Pp

Qq Rr Ss Tt

Uu Vv Ww Xx

Yy Zz